Marriage

A Revised *Betrayal of Sacred Trust*

Barbara Stuart

2013

Marriage

A Revised *Betrayal of Sacred Trust*

Living with an Unfaithful Husband

You are Special

Think of yourself as the most beautiful
Rose in the garden;
The calm ripple in the river;
The soft wave of the sea;
Your favourite colour in the rainbow;
The delicate sunrise in the east;
The beautiful sunset in the west;
The soft gentle dew on the grass;
The unique snowflake that gently falls to the
ground;
You are the most beautiful person created by God.
You are special
Because God created you different from everyone
else.

Marriage

A Revised *Betrayal of Sacred Trust*

Living With an Unfaithful Husband

Copyright © 2010 by B.Y. Stuart
First Published 2005
Second Publication 2010

Printed in the United States of America
ISBN 1453675728

A Note to Readers

Marriage is a Revised ***Betrayal of Sacred Trust*: *Living with an Unfaithful Husband***.

Betrayal of Sacred Trust will help the reader gain information concerning the marital relationship. It will reveal truths and pitfalls about marriage showing how easily an inconsiderate relationship can destroy what has taken a lifetime to build.

This book is ideal for lecturers involved in Women's Affairs, and has been used in premarital and marriage counseling.

The names used in *Betrayal of Sacred Trust* are fictitious. References made are similar to issues found in marriages and do not refer directly to particular persons.

The data from the study were changed to hide identities, geographic locations, ethnic, religious, and educational backgrounds.

Scripture references used in *Betrayal of Sacred Trust* are from the Holy Bible, King James Version.

Some verses were paraphrased for clarity, and not actual. Therefore, citations are at the end of related sentences.

Barbara Stuart
2010

Other Publications

For other books by this Author go to
www.themarriagecorner.web.officelive.com

Grace: *God's Unmerited Favour*
The Power of Prayer
Managing Difficult People
What is Love?
The Spirit of Jezebel in the Church: *The Big Façade*
Spiritual Warfare: *Setting Captives Free*
Principles of Spiritual Leadership
Ten Questions to ask myself before I say I DO
Fruit of the Spirit
Fruitfulness
The Chosen Vessel
Workplace Emotional Abuse
When the Circle Breaks: *Marital Unfaithfulness*

Table of Contents

Acknowledgements

The writing of *Betrayal of Sacred Trust* was not an exercise I envisioned when I first set out to do the research. Unfortunately, I could not extend the number of participants beyond the sample who came from various ethnic, social, geographical, and educational backgrounds.

To those persons I owe a deep depth of gratitude, and I again say thanks. There were contributions from others with vignettes that supported the theme and essence of the book, and I say thanks to them too.

To my sons, John-Paul, and Stephen, who encouraged me, and to my friends, I say thanks to all of you.

If there are any persons I have not recognized, and who should have been noted this is an over-sight and not intentional.

Finally, I owe everything to God who has given me the strength and courage to write at such a time in my life.

Preface

The presentation of *Betrayal of Sacred Trust* to the world is a contribution to complement texts that deal with women's affairs. The theme of the book is about marriage, infidelity, and interpersonal conflict.

The main intention for this book is to motivate the public and church leaders to make them become aware of the destructive nature of infidelity.

Additionally, the aim is to reveal the mental anguish infidelity cause to those women who choose to hold on to their sacred marriage vows.

This book is not the ultimate concerning women's issues since there are many other issues not covered in its contents. However, the hope is that the information is used where women's issues are discussed.

Betrayal of Sacred Trust represents all women everywhere whatever echelon of society: religious, educational, or social prominence.

This is a book about women, who have suffered physical abuses, the invisible wounds of emotional abuse, and the consequences from those situations.

For the sake of clarity, the concepts *adultery, unfaithfulness, cheating,* and *infidelity* are used alternatively in this book.

Introduction

For the past few decades, there has been a drastic transformation in the institution of marriage. This change has revolutionized its structure and stability, replacing it with various types of wanton and immoral behaviours. Not many generations ago, marriage was a safe and secure social structure. However, the increasing rise in sexual immorality has weakened this once strong foundation for family life.

On the pages of this book are the lives of women who have experienced the contagious social disease of adultery. It is contagious because it has become a social epidemic that has affected many families, broken many homes, and killed many relationships.

Marriage: *Betrayal of Sacred Trust,* unveils the lives of women who have made the decision to remain in marriages even though there were evidences of adultery. It uncovers the consequences of adultery, and describes the challenges some wives face who remain with their unfaithful husbands.

In some cases, the behaviour is active, whilst in others it has ceased or has become less frequent. It is the stories of those women that will be on the pages of this book. However, I had to suppress most of the original interviews to hide the identities of the participants.

Although the book does not whip the perpetrators of adultery, it gives a view of what life is like for some wives who have made the decision to remain in a situation that is damaging to their health, emotions, spirit, and mind.

It is a book for women, about women. Even if a woman has not had this experience, there are other situations just as painful as infidelity. Therefore, the book is about my life, your life, and the lives of every woman who has a story to tell.

The women in this category were selected because their cases were interesting. Furthermore, since it would seem that they are a forgotten group both in the society and in the church community, it was time to give them a voice.

Surprisingly, although the men committed adultery, *some* women continued to feel love and sincere passion for them. Nevertheless, their loving feelings towards the men did not prevent them from exuding anger when the need arose in response to their pain, and the emotional abuse that caused the pain. My question was, "What hindered the women from divorcing their husbands when it was evident that they had committed adultery?

Sadly, despite the reasons why the women remained with their spouses and the vast amount of literature that exist about divorce, many studies have not explored deeply into the incidence of infidelity, and the reasons why some wives remain with their unfaithful husbands.

This lack of interest into such a critical area of women's affairs casts a dark shadow on the advocates for women's causes. Could this be a message to those faithful wives that it is their choice to remain with their unfaithful husbands, or their situation is not important for a research study?

Agreeably, it is the woman's choice to remain with the unfaithful spouse. However, there are consequences for every act, or decision. Usually, those consequences extend to dimensions not previously anticipated. In many cases, there is the consideration and welfare of young children and other important personal matters why divorce would not be realistic.

Primarily, my aim for the study was to get an understanding of the decision the women made to remain with their unfaithful husbands, since the incidence of divorce seems to be uncontrollable in society and even in the church community.

To the men who will read **Marriage**: *Betrayal of Sacred Trust,* your wife is part of your body. Do not abuse her. Love her as you love yourself. Treat her with tenderness, love, compassion, and respect.

If a husband desires to have a loving and receptive wife, then he has a duty to keep her happy and not to make her feel inferior to him, even though he might be highly educated or earning more money.

Part I

The Family

Except the Lord build the house, they labour in vain that build it: except the Lord keep the city, the watchman waketh but in vain (Psalm 127:1, KJV).

This section covers the following:
- An Overview of the Family
- Changes in the Family System
- Structure of a Healthy Family
- Strengthening the Structure
- Children need Positive Examples

Chapter 1
An Overview of the Family

Not too long ago, the family system was one of the strongest of human social arrangement. It gave shelter, protection, warmth, and comfort within its boundaries. Those families practiced decency and respect within the environment, with clear rules, boundaries, and discipline. Those firm structures produced children who were often well-adjusted citizens in their neighbourhoods, and later became successful men and women.

History will relate to the results of strong families that produced lawyers, doctors, teachers, carpenters, architects, engineers, ministers, politicians and so on. This only indicates that a secure family structure builds a strong nation with adults who are confident and God-fearing with morals and social etiquette.

The first family began when God made Adam and gave him authority in the Garden of Eden to take charge of His creation (See Genesis 1-2). Later, He gave Adam Eve as his wife. The intention was for the couple to set up the first family system.

With this in mind, we can assume that the relationship of the couple was for companionship, intimacy, communication, procreation and all those elements that make up a happy contended family. This was the beginning of what is known in social science as the "family system." It means that each member is dependent upon the other; therefore when there are problems the entire system will be affected.

A typical system consists of parents and children who relate to each other through language, emotions, and various forms of communication signals. It is through this medium of communication that each member connects with the other and share hurts, grief, losses, successes, and life changing events. In such a setting, one will find laughter, joy, and various kinds of exchange as is found in a warm group formation.

Nevertheless, although there is the desire to maintain a firm moral foundation for their children, parents face very strong opposing forces that affect the moral development of their families. Those forces often make parents become lapse in their duties, resulting in the children making wrong decisions that leave them deluded and disappointed.

Eventually, the result of those situations erodes the family structure causing frustration, pain and various kinds of hurt. Often, it is from some of those early childhood experiences that the birth of domestic violence emerges.

Despite the problems that those parents faced, they were resilient and able to recover from disappointments and misfortunes. A strong family does not always mean that they are financially secure.

On the contrary, many of those families were only eking out from their small earnings to make a living. What made the difference is that each one supported the other, and this gave them determination to fight the odds, and go on to a life of success.

Moreover, many single mothers have had to go it alone without a father figure in the home, and often with only one job. Yet, they brought up children of whom they are proud. Many of those families came from the projects, and drug-ridden neighbourhoods.

The difference is that although they lived in the midst of crimes, they did not allow those situations to get into their homes. It must have been hard work.

Nevertheless, the efforts they made paid off in the end. I do not believe that where someone lives should be the deciding factor for the future. Besides, while someone may face setbacks, those situations should not cause the individual to remain in conditions that are detrimental to the goals and desires for making life better.

Chapter 2
Changes in the Family System

Unquestionably, we can all see that family life has changed tremendously over the generations. Although it was once a strong viable unit with morals and values for a solid and impressive relationship, those qualities are almost non-existent in many homes. The way in which parents individually and collective go after materialism, has choked the values once placed on family life.

Still, with this great background of morals and strength, what has happened down through the generations to make the family system one of the weakest structures in this millennium?

What source of power has undermined its strength and distorted the concept of family life? The evident weakness has resulted in the estrangement of children and parents, often the result of divorce, separation, or abuse in the home either between spouses or from parent to child.

Appropriately, Ekstrom & Roberto (1992) affirmed that, "Family life and traditional religious values were once the glue that naturally held people together. They were the roots in our society."

The writers further state, "In pursuing personal goals and material wealth, families and groups in our culture are not united as meaningfully as they could be" (p.4).

Obviously, these statements are evidence showing the breakdown in the framework of the family as values slowly disappear through greed, and the quest for more personal fulfillment at the expense of moral and religious standards. It is so disappointing to note that there are parents who find it quite comfortable to spend all day on Sunday at home watching the television, with sporting activities and other recreational interests, rather than taking their children to church.

Undoubtedly, there is the bombardment of an array of sophisticated mosaic devices, disguised in the cellophane of delusion, decorated with the tactics and strategies of the devil, and supported by the stimulus of worldly wisdom.

Additionally, with the open display of uncensored television programs portraying faulty methods of behaviours that incite violence in the home, there is certainly reason for alarm. This violence can be against children or between parents and/or significant others.

Ultimately, violence in the home leads to various kinds of abuses – physical, emotional, verbal, psychological, physiological, spiritual, and financial. Unmistakably, the result will lead to marital unfaithfulness.

Surprisingly, when one parent commits adultery, the erroneous belief is that the behaviour will not affect anyone else. This is so far from the truth. Adultery creates a chain reaction that touches everyone in the family, even the in-laws.

Consequently, we cannot minimize the fact that satanic influence is at the root of the breakdown of family life. He is the instigator for the violence and abuses that have become national concerns with the breakdown of marriages, and the death of so many mothers. For these reasons, every couple must seek to maintain order and self-control for a stable family life.

Therefore, we must make every effort to recapture the true meaning of *family*. We can all agree that a firm family structure is important because it produces positive well-rounded citizens, a good community, and a strong nation.

Chapter 3
Strengthening the Structure

Social scientists recognize the family as a system with three subsystems: parent-parent, parent-child, and siblings. Other smaller subsystems include extended relations. Each family has a set of rules to "enable each member to learn what is permitted or expected of him or her as well as others in the family transactions."[1]

Moreover, in a healthy structure, there is clear definition of roles, explanation of rules, the sharing of power between parents as they take the leading roles, while the children follow accordingly with the understanding of what each has to do. Clearly, if each member knows, understands, and accepts those rules there will be harmony in the home.

In addition, the power lines function through an open effective communication system. There is respect for each other with effective feedback, love, laughter, and all the dynamics for free flow of expressions that lead to homeostasis in the system.

It is the rules that clarify acceptable behaviours among family members. Therefore, when parents breach the very rules they have set, the children become confused and frustrated with disappointment. Those children will be anxious because they are not sure what to do, or what to believe.

The assumption here is that when parents violate their own codes of behaviour that are emotionally destructive, then children lose respect for them. It is so despicable to hear parents using foul language to their children, and the children echoing equally to them.

---

[1] From Goldenberg & Goldenberg, *Family Therapy*, 3d.ed. (Brooks/Cole Publishing Company, Pacific Grove, CA, 1991), 36.

Violation of family rules by parents will affect the attitudes and behaviours of children, and this comes through the communication system, even without a spoken word.

In contrast, in an unhealthy family system, you will find evidences of dysfunctional behaviour patterns. In such a home, there is rigidity, mixed or unclear communication, with fear among the members.

Usually, the one who assumes the greatest power/status exercises a strong arm with an iron rod that wields incessantly against the other members in the home. Children are often fearful, and the mother had better be quiet even against physical abuse, and incest.

Rarely do children in an unhealthy home have the opportunity to own pets or bring friends home. Unlike the open system, the occupants do not know the beauty of living in an emotionally warm environment where there is peace, joy, and love.

Sadly, those children who have witnessed negative behaviours in the home will follow the examples of their parents. Therefore, if the parents are kind to each other; then the children will do likewise. If they fight and swear at each other, the same behaviours will be emulated between siblings, parent and child, and even on the outside.

Communication

In order to maintain a strong structure, there must be an active communication process. This includes feedback, which gives an indication of the types of response each member in the family displays, whatever the circumstances might be.

Furthermore, feedback is necessary because parents and children will be aware of acceptable behaviours, and the ones that are destructive and unacceptable. The process of feedback must be active, and should not prevent any member from expressing likes and dislikes concerning what works and what does not. This means each person takes time to listen to the other so that the process of communication remains open.

There must be open dialogue and exchange of ideas and opinions. The responses from the feedback system will bring about changes, correct wrongs, and improve weaknesses. However, if there are blockages in the system the result is stagnation in communication with constant emotional discomfort in the home.

In a closed system which is harsh and inflexible, the activity of feedback is restricted. In that type of unhealthy structure, all rules are mandatory with no questions asked. Therefore, it is difficult for members to express grievance or seek for explanation of rules.

For example, "daddy why can't I..." the response might be "because I say so." Hence, when rules are set in place no one dares question them. Instead, each person must obey, and any infraction is disastrous to the one who is at fault.

Roles

In the typical home, we have the father and mother and they each have significant roles mandated by God for each other, and for the family. The roles incorporates love, nurturing, emotional support, social, moral, spiritual, and practical training for their children. If either of these two persons fail to carry out their God-given responsibilities this is sinful and leads to rebellion against God.

Moreover, the children will be led astray and they might learn obnoxious and deviant behaviours from people who themselves are God-less, antisocial, and immoral. Therefore, when the home life is disturbed because of infidelity, the children are confused and they take their hostilities away from the home, to church, to school, into the neighbourhood, and even into adulthood.

Some children repress their feelings and this is even worse for them because they are hurting on the inside. Possibly, many times when a child misbehaves, the root cause comes from the home. The symptoms can lead to a parent who is not carrying out parental responsibilities or is negligent in doing so. This does not mean that all detestable behaviours are lack of parental guidance.

In any case, the very social system can become an enemy to the parents because they can no longer discipline their children the way generations before once did. The result is that parents have lost control over their children because of the influence of certain faulty theories from ideologists. Let me explain, nothing is wrong with any method of discipline, so long as it does not interfere with the social, godly, and moral life of children.

Discipline

In many homes today the structure, if there is one, maybe disorder and godlessness. There is permissiveness while parents are busy about their own affairs. Every child needs structure, and discipline is a developmental tool that is necessary for parents to use in teaching their children acceptable social behaviours. If there is no discipline, then that child lives in a lax environment.

The Bible states, *"The rod and reproof give wisdom: but a child left to himself brings his mother to shame"* (Proverbs 29:15). This point needs no discussion because the news media display the violent behaviours of the youth every day.

The rod of reproof does not mean abuse of any kind, or even corporal punishment. What it really means is that a child needs discipline when he/she does something that is wrong. I must say here that discipline is not punishment. Instead, it is another way in which the parent tells a child "I love you and desire for you to behave appropriately, whether I am present or away from you."

Although some theorists do not believe that children need spanking, yet there are times when a short smart in the right place will do more good than facing the wall. Most of the successful men and women today will attest to the fact that they had some type of discipline in their youth. Those restraints and corrections kept them out of places, and situations that would have only brought shame and disgrace to them and their parents.

Undoubtedly, there is a real enemy and he wants to control the minds of everyone including children. He has taken over the conscience of society, and today, the nation and the world are reaping the harvest of the evils sown. I will repeat children need discipline in their lives to guide them.

Discipline helps to maintain a firm structure in the home. While parents purchase exotic gifts, expensive toys, and give children vacations in far off places; those things are good and have their places.

Likewise, a home might be in the most elaborate upper-class neighbourhood, and equipped with all kinds of expensive appliances to make life happy for the family. Yet, there is no guarantee that children will grow with the morals and confidence they need without a firm set of discipline.

Nevertheless, the only thing the children might remember is the way the parents took time to teach them positive social behaviours. Children will remember the discipline they received from their parents because they have shaped their lives. Later, they are able to teach their children to be successful citizens in the society.

Finally, I must interject that discipline does not mean demeaning a child or treating one different from the other. Children need love, and this must be without partiality among them. Parents must be careful to be fair with the way they issue discipline to their children.

Chapter 4
Children Need Positive Examples

Children are impressionable and therefore, open to all kinds of behavioural patterns displayed before them. Consequently, when parents have disputes with each other, they should not involve the children to cause them pain and heartache. It is sad to note, that very often the disputing parties do not think about the consequences of their actions in the home.

Any immoral act performed by a member in the home or by a close relative, and viewed by children can affect the moral structure of the family. Young children copy what they see, while older children may confront the offender [parent] to obtain answers for inappropriate behaviours.

If proper examples are not set before children, they will emulate the behaviours they see in their immediate environment as the right thing to do. This means that if the children are aware that mom or dad is behaving in a manner that is unusual with someone of the opposite sex, this will make them unhappy and disappointed.

Those children will become disturbed because they no longer know what to believe. Furthermore, when the marriage breaks down it is easy for them to think that it is their fault that mom and dad do not love each other anymore. It may seem inconceivable, but some parents do view children as obstacles when they decide to carry out their schemes to cheat on one another.

Seemingly, many parents fail to realize that children are very impressionable and they take things very seriously. Therefore, if one parent uses a child against the other, this can be detrimental with lasting effects that will follow even into adulthood. In any case, children want to know that they are safe, and that they will always have their parents with them.

Obviously, infidelity has placed a dent into the structure of the family making marriages very tenuous. I wonder if parents should prepare children that one day mom and dad might divorce if they do not love each other anymore. This thought may sound extreme. Nevertheless, maybe parents should prepare children for the inevitable in marriages due to its uncertainty in this age.

The sad part is when parents *know* there is no hope of the marriage ever coming back together again, yet they lie to children and on one another. They blame each other and still put up a front before their children. How long can this go on? Eventually those children are able to arrive at a conclusion with an understanding of the facts as they grow older.

Effect of Negative Examples

Children's perception of problems in the home will often make them feel sorrow, grief, and disappointment. They can experience those feelings when their parents' divorce each other, or when they cross the line and cheat on one another.

When this happens, many children become depressed, inattentive in school, and sometimes they will display unusual behavioural problems both in school and at home.

One does not need to argue that a survey is hardly required to accept the fact that a firm and stable marriage builds a strong family. This includes children who will possess a high degree of self-concept, moral dignity, and a solid spiritual foundation. Again, it is from this structure that a strong community and nation emerge.

Despite this universal knowledge about the importance of a godly marriage and its influence on family life, its structure has become so fragile, that some couples seem to be opting for "as long as we *love* each other," instead of "'til death us do part." Parents must understand that when there are problems in the home, the children are adversely affected. For many parents when they discover their error, it is too late.

The home should be a place of safety, yet so many children experience and witness physical and emotional abuses.

Let all parents take heed concerning the way they treat their children and the types of behaviours they display before them.

Chapter 5
Influences on the Family

The Society

There are parents who are facing challenges rearing their children with the new principles conjured up by society, gleaned from psychological ideologists, who pose as the supreme knowledge and authority in opposition to the Word of God.

Some of those ideologies are for the most part completely distant from Biblical principles used over time for a Christ-centred home. This is where the fear of God is present; and children learn respect for others, the self, property, and the law from their parents. From the early years those children learn to reverence God and about His character.

One reason why the family system has weakened is that sincere fidelity in marriage is lacking by the examples shown in some homes. The very concept of fidelity in marriage has become unconvincing even in the church community.

It seems that some people are quite comfortable to consider divorce as the *only* means to heal a sick marriage. Statistics [*not available*] have reported that there are as many or even more divorces coming out of the church in comparison to mainline society. If this is true, then it is time for the church and society to become aware.

It is inescapable, that if the institution of marriage which is the main foundation for effective family life fails, it will present clear evidence that the strength of the family will continue to deteriorate.

Moreover, there are all kinds of influences, which threaten marriages and eventually the structure for the family. For example, today we hear of alternate life-style, same-sex marriages, gender changes, and trial marriages – which is shacking up; and some will tell you outright that marriage is not necessary because it is only a piece of paper.

With those societal influences, what is the solution to the new ideologies that have invaded the minds of people anesthetizing and lulling them to sleep? How can we take back our families held captives in those types of iron-grid theoretical manacles? Clearly, society has certainly changed the family structure by accepting what used to be forbidden and thus, tainting the godly concept of the meaning of family.

The Church

Regrettably, the truth is that some churches no longer preach against sin because they do not use the word in the pulpit. Otherwise, they may lose members, the financial resources may decrease; or it is no longer fashionable [politically correct] to use such a term. Those situations give clear evidence that the church has failed in its mission to the world.

The commission Jesus gave before He left was, *"Go ye therefore, and teach all nations...to observe all things whatsoever I have commanded you:"* (Matthew 28:19-20). In Acts 1:9, Jesus said *"But ye shall receive power, after that the Holy Ghost is come upon you: and ye shall be witnesses unto me...and unto the uttermost part of the earth."*

My questions are, "Where is the power?" "What are we doing with it?" What is the church teaching?" "Where is the witness?" It is possible that many people will agree that the first place majority of parents took their newborn, was to the church for the pastor's blessings. If this is so, "Why are there so many broken families because of divorce?" What is most disturbing is that, apparently Christians do not commit sin anymore. Instead, they make mistakes.

Both inside and outside of the church sin is now dressed up in the most expensive glamorous clothing, decked with the latest fashionable jewelry, and supported by watered-down messages that lack power, substance, and effect.

Most young people avoid going to church, even those who are professed Christians because they are bored. Admittedly, some preachers do go on *automatic* power with boring tailored sermons with no unction from the Holy Spirit. Where is the power? Where is the effect of the Holy Spirit? It is time to wake up and recognize that the church has failed. Unmistakably, if the church has failed, there will be failure in the family that will affect the community, and nation.

Gender Exchange

Another skew to the breakdown of the traditional family structure is that some husbands, and even wives, are leaving their spouses for the same sex. In some situations, men have left their wives for other men/women, and wives for other women/men. Those behaviours are destroying the true meaning of marriage and family life, leaving children even more disturbed than before.

If the institution of marriage becomes defenseless to the changes in society then this will greatly affect the structure of the family.

Here is a comparison of a healthy home, and a dysfunctional home.

A Healthy Home is   *A Dysfunctional Home is*

Secure, loving, peaceful with joy, laughter, and happiness

Constantly in chaos Secure with material things

Friendly, trusting; with loyalty, respect, and fellowship

Frequently hostile; with fear, and anger

Built with humility, forgiveness, and integrity

Built with pride, arrogance, and deceit

Peaceful with harmony and order

Filled with turmoil and confusion

Has God as Leader

God-less, money is power in that home

Governed by godly precepts

Governed by worldliness

Constructive with positive problem solving skills

Destructive with the use of negative problem solving skill

Part II
Marriage

And the LORD God said, "It is not good for the man to be alone. I will make a companion who will help him" (Genesis 2:18, KJV).

This section covers the following:
- God's Plan for Marriage
- Responsibilities of Husband and Wife
- Important Features of the Relationship
- Effective Communication
- Maintaining Sexuality
- Factors that Influence Marriage
- The Future of Marriage
- The Modern View of Marriage
- The Christian Marriage
- Preserving the Relationship
- Marriage Requires Hard Work
- Why They Remained

Chapter 6
God's Plan for Marriage

It is clear to see the moral decadence in society and its influence on family life since most marriages are not lasting as long as they did many years ago. However, despite the weaknesses in marriage, there are people who still hold the Christian marriage sacredly as the only means of securing a stable, godly, and moral family structure. Contrastingly, there are others with different beliefs concerning marriage that are a threat to the standards laid down by God.

According to God's plan, marriage is a covenant relationship with one man and one woman divinely instituted to bring happiness, procreation of godly children, and to avoid immorality. Hence, marriage, similar to all other relationships, requires a structural framework that is secure and strong upon which to build a stable home. The assumption is that the structure of marriage needs the basis of a firm belief and confident relationship with the Supreme God through Jesus Christ.

Therefore, the couple must have shared interests and goals, good communication patterns, common religious faith, continuous fidelity, and the ability to settle interpersonal conflicts in a non-violent, harmonious fashion for permanence and stability of the relationship.

Besides, it is also important for the persons who are planning to marry to have clear knowledge of the structure of marriage. This is important because many persons enter into this institution with unrealistic expectations and selfish ideologies that are impossible for anyone to meet or accept. Obviously, each partner comes with personal needs that are emotional, psychological, social, spiritual, and financial.

Naturally, if any one of those needs is unmet, this can cause a breakdown early in the relationship. When it happens, attitudes begin to change and the expressions of emotions are often in angry unfriendly ways. Conflicts do not come from out of the air. There is always a reason for unfriendly behaviours whether real or unreal.

Some marriages break because the couple was unprepared for the life changes that two people bring to make a whole. There are identity collisions in some cases, while in others the expectations go beyond the realities.

Some of the factors in God's plan that make up a strong marriage include the following:

Faithfulness

The teachings of the Bible place strong emphasis on marital faithfulness because the Christian marriage is an institution sealed by a covenant. God requires faithfulness by the partners even in the face of adversities, which are not crucial or destructive to the life of any one.[2]

The principle of faithfulness is an indication to the permanence of marriage based on firm standards of tenderness, unfailing love, integrity, honesty, and loyalty. These are fundamental qualities that are vital for the stability of the marriage, including faith, and the help of the Holy Spirit.

Many times personality collision comes in the first six months when the two people are learning about each other's differences and peculiarities; likes and dislikes; weaknesses and strengths; and idiosyncrasies that were not visible during the time of courtship.

During that time of testing, they will need God's help to *instruct, teach* and *guide* them (Psalm 32:8) through this rough path into the unknown. Those early days are like treading into dangerous territories.

Moreover, the couple must pray and read the Bible together as they get to know each other. They also need much patience to guide them through this wilderness of experience. If the correct patterns are set at

---

[2] From S.J. Mikolaski, (1992). *Encyclopedia of Christian Ethics.* Revised edition, R. K. Harrison (ed.). (Thomas Nelson Publishers, 1992), pp.144-146.

the initial stage, and there is unity, there is a better chance for the stability and permanence of the marriage.

Plainly, faithfulness is a major factor in the relationship requiring people who possess wisdom, strength, courage, faith, perseverance, and a positive self-concept to maintain this component for the life of the relationship. There should also be mutual agreement for truthfulness and trustworthiness with a sincere desire for fidelity, loyalty, cooperation, and love.

Incidentally, faithfulness does not *only* mean a marriage free from adultery. This concept goes much further and extends throughout the relationship.[3] Faithfulness also includes not withholding sexual intimacy, and providing financial security.

It also means a marriage free of all types of abuses inflicted by one partner upon the other. Abuse does not only mean physical; but mental, emotional, spiritual, and psychological.

Spiritual Unity

Essentially, both partners should be members of the Body of Jesus Christ. This means that they are born again through baptism, with control of the in-dwelling Holy Spirit. They must have a willingness to live out the Christian life in peace and harmony together. The Bible is strictly against a believer marrying a non-believer, that is, someone who has not been born again.[4]

Mutual spiritual unity from the biblical perspective is an integral segment of the couple's responsibilities, and crucial for the life of the marriage. The reason why this is so important is that, if the two people belong to the same denomination, there is the likelihood that they will have fewer problems concerning doctrinal beliefs. It does make a

---

[3] See *When the Circle Breaks: Marital Unfaithfulness* @ www.themarraigecorner.web.officelive.com

[4] Be ye not unequally yoked together with unbelievers: for what fellowship hath righteousness with unrighteousness? And what communion hath light with darkness (II Corinthians 6:14).

difference when there is spiritual unity since they will each understand what is required of them as a couple.

Additionally, they might have fewer problems in the way they rear their children. Indeed, spiritual mutuality is one of the most vital components and significant in every marriage where partners are submissive to God's plan for building a strong marriage.

Compatibility

Let us eavesdrop on a conversation.

Husband: I did not know that you do not like to go out.

Wife: But I thought you knew.

Husband: How was I supposed to know? You never told me. We used to be out regularly and you seemed to have enjoyed those times.

Wife: Do I have to tell you everything? You are the one with the PhD.

Husband: What does my degree have to do with anything?

Wife: You must have noticed how quickly I became bored and wanted to go home.

Husband: Well, I thought you were just tired, or had a headache or something. I cannot read your mind.

Wife: I did not ask you to read my mind. All I want is for you to understand me…

After reading the script above you may have noticed that neither of the two was listening to the other; neither did they know much about each other. Compatibility is one of the major elements for careful consideration when planning a marriage.

While couples will make the financial plans for their wedding including all the attendants who will be present, what many partners fail to do is to make the effort to find out about each other's likes and dislikes. No two persons are alike, not even identical twins.

The fact is that God uniquely makes everyone with specific personality components. Some individuals like to be with many people, and they are the life of the party. Others are comfortable with only a few, mainly their close family and friends. Still, there are those who prefer to be alone most of the time because they are moody or they just prefer their own company.

Therefore, before couples decide to make the lifetime commitment to marry, it would be wise to ensure mutual agreement concerning the things and activities that give them pleasure. Trying to make changes after the marriage only brings disappointment and sorrow in many situations.

Another significant point is that the couple should find out what type of temperament each partner has because this information will help in their relationship together. In the scene above, the husband seemed to be of a sanguine personality who likes going out, while his wife who might be of a melancholy type, prefers to stay home.

There is also another extremely important point that needs consideration before the couple makes the decision to marry. Many individuals have set times for starting a family.

Therefore, the couple should discuss each other's views concerning whether or not they will have children. Essentially, they should not take each other for granted thinking that because they are married, each of them is ready to begin a family immediately after the wedding.

After Jan and Maurice were married, she decided that she was ready to have a child without even discussing her decision with him beforehand. In her mind, she thought he was just as ready and excited to begin their family, but she was wrong. However, she became pregnant a few months after the wedding, Maurice was furious. According to her, that was the point where the marriage began to crumble.

Continues in the next chapter.

Chapter 7
God's Plan for Marriage
[Part 2]

Trust

One of the most important building blocks in a marital relationship is trust. It is a requirement, which means firmness, honesty, loyalty, and integrity. Trust will be one of the basic factors for resolving broken relationship especially after infidelity. The reason is that the discovery of infidelity will shatter trust in a marriage that may have taken many years to build.

This means that one or both partners have broken what seemed to have been a solid relationship. To re-build trust, the partners will have to change their negative thinking about each other (*see* Philippians 4:8), as well as the negative behaviours that may have caused the break in the relationship.

Trust means having confidence and reliance on the other party in a relationship for consistency, truthfulness, dependability, and sincerity. Therefore, if a wife forgives her husband after he has promised her that he will not repeat his adulterous behaviours, the onus is on him to maintain and keep his promise as she tries to re-build her confidence in his love for her.

Finally, both partners must trust each other with the belief that they will uphold the values and principles of the marital relationship. It makes no sense lying to each other or making promises that are only hollow words. If the marriage is going to last it takes the efforts of both partners to rely on each other to maintain fidelity, commitment, and all the other components that are necessary for the upkeep and permanence of the relationship.

Empathy

God's plan also means that the couple will be empathetic towards each other. The reason is that empathy is one of those qualities that will enhance the promotion of a positive interpersonal relationship and in the healing of broken relations.

The story Jesus told of the Good Samaritan is an excellent example of showing empathy (Luke 10:29-37), particularly in the case of a repentant adulterer. It takes someone with deep feelings to help another who needs support even if the individual did something wrong that got him in trouble. The story shows where empathy went beyond the limits of selfishness, and plunges beneath faults to lift the burden of sorrow in order to help an injured person.

Therefore, when an adulterous husband returns to his wife and asks forgiveness, she should see him as a wounded soul needing help rather than accuse, criticize, and ignore him. Do not get me wrong. She needs to express her feelings; but there is a time for that when she can do so without causing more damage.

The Good Samaritan did not ask for explanations. He was thoughtful and considerate of the injured man's suffering. Without doubt, it must have been the awareness of pain and hurt from the evident wounds that made him bend to clean the wounds, pick up the injured man, put him on his donkey, and take him to a safe place.

Moreover, empathy will ultimately replace aggression with love, and peace with hostilities. Empathy is naturally showing sensitivity because it means walking in the other person's shoes, and feeling with that person.

The Scriptures state that love covers a multitude of sin.[5] Consequently, if the adulterer is truly sorrowful, it presents an opening for the stronger person to restore the other to the relationship.

---

[5] See 1 Peter 4:8

Accordingly, there must also be time to listen to the other person. Usually, it is not so much what one person says, but what he/she did not say that triggers interest to the reality of what is going on in the life of the other individual. Here is where the other person's attention maybe won. Sometimes the body language will capture the attention of the listener that will create an opportunity for explanations.

Commitment

With the rise in divorces and the pervasiveness of extramarital activities, commitment to marriage has become outdated in most social arenas. It is usual to hear of the various times individuals have been married, and the number of ex-spouses and children they have left in their paths.

Nevertheless, God's plan is for both individuals to remain together throughout the relationship. The marriage vows say, "'til death us do part." However, one of the reasons why most couples opt for divorce is the well-known clause in Matthew 19:9, where Jesus said, "...*Whosoever shall put away his wife, except it be for fornication,...*"

Still, many churches do not uphold the "except" concept, but refer to Paul's teachings on marriage and separation (*See* I Corinthians 7). Regardless of the option for divorce, commitment to marriage is vital for the longevity of the relationship.

Despite its importance, not everyone is willing to adhere to the principle of commitment. Instead, some people both in and out of the church adopt the butterfly model of going from flower to flower, sipping unfamiliar nectar to satisfy their ego and sexual desires.

Those persons are not willing to make a firm commitment to the standards for a permanent monogamous relationship. The understanding concerning commitment is that God's objective was a distinct command for unity, the building of a stable relationship, procreation, sincere trust, and devotion to each other

Furthermore, when partners are fully committed to the sanctity of marriage and are in obedience to God's plan, they will endeavour to comply with the requirements of a committed relationship. They will carry out their obligations and devotion towards each other with loyalty and faithfulness to the vows they made to each other before God and witnesses.

It is true that one partner may profess that he/she has not committed adultery, and therefore, that is commitment to the marriage; even so, adultery is not the *only* factor that will affect the relationship. This, I would say is the ultimate because it breaks the sacred covenant bond between two persons united in the presence of God in holy matrimony.

Most emphatically, commitment means recognizing that the marriage bed *must* remain undefiled and off limits to anyone else other than one's spouse. The preservation of fidelity, dedication, and integrity are indications of true marital commitment.

It is sincere commitment that will keep the bonds of marital unity together when crises occur in the relationship. Crises are sometimes unavoidable and they will test the strength and character of the partners. It does not matter what the crises might be they do appear.

What is most important about crises is whether the marriage will last the duration of the test. This is a crucial factor to take into consideration because it is at such times that the faith and love of the couple are tested. Each trying event in the marriage might seem to be the end.

Commitment in those times means keeping the promise to "love, honour, and obey; in sickness and in health; for richer or poorer; 'til death us do part" no matter what happens, yet *within the scope of human endurance*. Commitment is part of God's plan for a wholesome marital relationship.

Chapter 8
Responsibilities of Husband and Wife

The success of any marriage depends on the effective working together of both husband and wife. It means that they should each assume specific responsibilities set out by God for the permanence and quality of the marriage.[6] The factor of responsibility in the marriage for husband and wife is not a gender-marked-role-identity. Rather, it is an integral aspect of the relationship mandated by God since creation for harmony and stability in the home.

The Husband

It is evident that from the beginning of time, God's intention was for the man to be the leader in the home. Unto the woman He said, *"thy desire shall be to thy husband, and he shall rule over you"* (Genesis 3:16). *Hold it!* This does not mean that the wife is inferior to her husband. It certainly does not mean that the husband should have dominion over his wife as an authority figure or a dictator, nor should he abuse her in any way.

The husband's responsibility is in comparison to the relationship of Christ and the Church. In Ephesians 5:25-33 the Bible teaches,

"Husbands, love your wives, even as Christ also loved the church, and gave himself for it." The Bible further adds that, *"…men ought to love their wives as their own bodies. He that loveth his wife loveth himself."*

"Husbands, love your wives, and be not bitter against them" (Colossians 3:19).

Peter further emphasized stating, *"Likewise, ye husbands, dwell with them according to knowledge, giving honour unto the wife, as unto the*

---

[6] See Ephesians 5:22-33

weaker vessel, and as being heirs together of the grace of life; that your prayers be not hindered" (I Peter 3:7).

This love does not mean empty talk, or the making of unrealistic promises. It is the kind of love stated in I Corinthians 13:4-7. This love is forgiving and does not keep scores of infractions. Instead, this kind of love displays truthfulness and honesty for each other. The man who loves his wife as his own body will not commit adultery, abuse her in any way, or coerce her into taking part in unnatural and immoral sexual activities.

Referring to the analogy of Christ and the church, husbands should be devoted to their wives with willingness to treat them with respect and high regard as they, too, wish to be treated.

Another responsibility of the husband is to hold the marriage together as he cleaves to his wife in a loving relationship, and that he treats her as his own body. Absolutely, if a man adheres to the principles, there will be no space for infiltration of anything foreign that will cause pain or grief.

The main role for the husband is to be leader in the home. What is marital leadership? This is simple to understand. Similar to how one foot must go before the other to convey the body, so it is in the marital relationship. There must be order and unity.

Each partner has a role, but someone must lead and that is the duty of the husband. If the wife is unwilling to accept her husband as leader, then the institution of marriage is not for her.

The Wife

The Bible clearly defines the responsibilities of the wife, stating that she should readily acknowledge the leadership of her husband as his helper (Genesis 2:18; Colossians 3:18; I Peter 3:1-6). Hence, the wife ought to be in submissiveness to her husband by respecting his leadership,[7] if she intends to be in obedience to God and His plan for marriage

---

[7] See Ephesians 5:22-24

Moreover, a wife who submits to her husband is promoting a loving and tender spirit through her faith and trust in the Lord. This can only happen if she depends on him to sustain her, even when she encounters difficult situations.[8]

Although feminist activists advocate outrageous rights for women, the Christian wife must not become confused with those ideas in order to conform to standards that will separate her from the presence of God and affect her obedience to Him. Therefore, she should not allow worldly ideologies to intimidate her, so that she is outside the will of the Lord because her obedience is not an indication of weakness.

Accordingly, the husband must not take God's Word out of context to suit his own selfish ideas, or to dominate his wife. While the Word of God states that the wife must be submissive, it does not mean domination.

Claire:

> I was newly married for the second time. Although my husband and I did not court for a long period, I knew that I loved him, and I thought he loved me, too. I had been widowed for a few years and felt that here was an opportunity to have a loving companion when I met Jack. He showed all the signs of being a good Christian. To my surprise, this was only a pretense. I soon discovered that he wanted me to be the replica of his wife who had died a few years earlier. When I refused to do what he wanted, such as wearing her clothes, and some other unreasonable things, he told me that I should be subject to him. *I do not believe this report needs any comment from me.*

In addition, the biblical teachings plainly show that the husband ought to cherish his wife, and esteem her more than he does with any other woman. Correspondingly, the wife's desire must *only* be to her own husband while he in turn *cleaves* to her, implying oneness with deep passion, devotion, nurturing, emotional intimacy, enduring love, and consistent support.

In order for the family to be healthy, both husband and wife must carry out their duties to be good parents before their children. Together

---

[8] Psalm 55:22

it is their responsibility to set healthy examples before them, which the children can duplicate later with their own families. It will be the positive examples of the parents that will give the children a sense of stability and security, and enhance their emotional health.

Besides, the children will be prone to obeying instructions (*See* Ephesians 6:1-4) when parents demonstrate the correct examples before them. This will help them to make wise decisions, and display acceptable social behaviours as they interact with their friends.

I wonder why some men find it so difficult to maintain their marital vows. Why do they cheat on their wives and in some cases act as though it is not a serious breach of their marital vows? It could be that ministers are no longer using the "ancient" words, which were once part of the marriage ceremony.

Therefore, if the partners did not believe they made a solemn commitment to love each other "'til death us do part, etc.," then the understanding might be to just do whatever pleases them, or walk out of the marriage when it does not work for them.

The responsibilities may seem to be an overwhelming challenge for the couple, yet with God's help, all things are possible and they *can* do *all* things through Christ, who will strengthen them.

Chapter 9
Important Features to the Relationship

Intimacy

When God ordained marriage, it was His intention that partners shared an intimate relationship with each other. For many couples, intimacy means only the physical expression of love. However, it represents much more than that aspect because intimacy transcends the physical demonstration, and refers to *oneness* in the marital relationship.

This oneness is a fellowship comparable only to Jesus Christ and the church.[9] Moreover, intimacy combines the emotional, physical, intellectual, sexual, and spiritual aspects of the marital relationship, "yet with a special oneness that demonstrates a healthy separateness."[10]

Further, the presence of intimacy helps to maintain the relationship as the couple confidently grows closer together with respect for each other. They learn to understand each other's foibles and the reasons for things that they did not understand.

Being Watchful

The responsibility of both husband and wife is to be vigilant so that satanic forces do not infiltrate the relationship. These come in all kinds of situations which are often unexpected.

Hence, it is important that they spend quality time together in prayer and devotion to prepare them to face the attacks and schemes of the enemy. Satan is an enemy who designs schemes to plant various destructive elements within the marital relationship leading to conflicts and discord. Peter describes him as a "roaring lion"[11] who is seeking

---

[9] Genesis 2:24; Matthew 19:5-6; Mark 10:6-8; Ephesians 5:22-33.
[10] From R.E Hawkins, *Strengthening Marital Intimacy*. (Baker Book House, 1991).
[11] 1 Peter 5

for his next prey. If the couple is not vigilant, some of the schemes the enemy uses to rupture the marital relationship are usually demonstrated in interpersonal conflicts.

If the couple becomes careless, the enemy will create havoc to the relationship. When he enters, his plan is to *steal* their peaceful rapport, *kill* their love for each other, and in some cases, *destroy* their marriage (*Compare* John 10:10).

On reflection, can we ascribe all the weaknesses to the enemy? He might try to destroy the relationship, but he can only do as much as the individuals allow him. In Luke 10:19 Jesus said *"Behold I give unto you power to tread on serpents and scorpions, and over all the power of the enemy: and nothing shall by any means hurt you."*

Therefore, although the enemy may have a scheme to destroy the relationship, the Holy Spirit can prevent his plan from taking place if the couple is vigilant to his devices.

For this reason, it is very important for the couple to walk in the Spirit (Galatians 5:16), who will protect them from danger (*See* Psalm 91:10), if they trust and allow Him to direct them. Obviously, the possession of the skills to resolve interpersonal conflicts in a positive and harmonious manner can be the crux for preserving the marriage.

Unfulfilled Expectations

Every partner brings some kind of expectations into the marriage. If any of them is unfulfilled, then the enemy uses the disappointment as an opportunity for the person in need to believe that the marriage is not working. That person might become irritable, frustrated, unhappy, and will complain because of the unfulfilled desires.

> For example, *Mary* came from a home where mom stayed home and dad worked. After she became pregnant, it was time to stay at home until the baby was born, and further still, until the child went to school. *Bill* was not prepared for this because he came from a working class family where *everyone* worked.

In another situation, the wife may have secret desires of her own for not wanting to go out to work because she believes that her husband should take care of all her needs. There are women who do believe that their husbands must "supply all their needs," whether they have riches stored somewhere or not.

Even though it is the husband's duty to provide for his wife and family, there are times when economic changes arise that will bring about financial distresses. Those situations are often unplanned eventualities, and they do cause disappointments and grief. It is possible that the partner who is less dedicated to the spiritual values of married life will quickly become disenchanted and less committed to the wishes of the other partner.

Therefore, it is fundamentally significant for both partners to firmly establish themselves in the Christian faith, with a strong and sincere relationship with the Lord Jesus Christ. Clearly, the need for spiritual mutuality is most important for the relationship to have any hope of survival, especially in an economic crisis.

Love Games

In this situation, if the needs of the partners are unmet, the quality of love might change because someone will be holding out against the other. Sometimes couples use sex as currency to play games if only to get what each wants or to spite the other person. Conditional love is a sign of instability in the relationship that will lead to insecurity between the partners.

For instance, when the expression of love is solely for the meeting of needs, if those needs are unmet, then the disappointed partner might be tempted to stray from the marriage bed. That person might only leave the bedroom, or sleep on the couch until the need is met one way or another.

In another situation, if the husband sees that his wife is not responding he will use her behaviour as reason to stray and find someone outside who will show love towards him.

However, the Bible states "*Marriage is honourable in all, and the bed undefiled: but whoremongers and adulterers God will judge*" (Hebrews 13:4). Therefore, the bed is off limits. This does not mean only the physical bed, but having sexual activities outside of one's spouse.

Despite evidence of adultery, the partners should both seek out professional counseling for reconciliation. This requires mutual understanding with a willingness to work through the problems and bring about the healing of the marriage. If one partner refuses to make love to the other this is unscriptural, and neither the wife nor the husband should behave in such a manner with each other. This withholding might lead to adultery. The Bible states:

> *Defraud ye not one the other, except it be with consent for a time, that ye may give yourselves to fasting and prayer; and come together again, that Satan tempt you not for your incontinency* (I Corinthians 7:12, KJV).

Fear

Insecurity will result in fear, which is one of the schemes the enemy uses to deceive at least one of the partners in believing that the marriage is not working. The Bible teaches that, *"There is no fear in love; but perfect love casts out fear"* (I John 4:18a). Obviously, when fear is present in the relationship there may be a tendency for flight. It is understandable that fear comes from the devil, but God gives the power to love, and soundness of mind (*See* I Timothy 1:7).

Unmistakably, infidelity is one of the situations that can create fear in the mind of the injured wife in many ways. She might be concerned about her physical safety, financial security, loss of control over the marriage, or even losing the children, and her home. Fear is indeed torment and holds the individual in a prison-like manner.

With fear comes suspicion. This is especially so, after the adulterer confesses and promises not to repeat the behaviour. The wife will feel insecure each time the husband is late coming home from work. She watches his every move and constantly asks questions concerning his whereabouts.

Fear is a controlling device that manipulates and keeps its victims in bondage. It is as if people in those situations feed themselves on fear. Moreover, fear eats away self-confidence and personal development because the person only believes negative things about the self and others. This debilitating emotion weakens an injured wife and prevents her from enjoying life.

Low Self-Esteem

When a wife finds out that her husband has cheated on her, she will become disheartened with disappointment and his lack of commitment. It is from this feeling of discouragement that often results in thoughts that bring on low self-esteem.

Unmistakably, the presence of low self-esteem is an enemy to intimacy resulting in low self-worth. It also brings doubt and mistrust into the relationship, and hinders personal growth and development. Besides, low self-esteem is one of the enemy's deadliest emotional and psychological weapons against a marriage that has been infected with the sin of adultery.

Low self-esteem destroys dreams and paralyzes potentials while it ruins relationships (Gregory, 1988). Further, to re-build self-esteem again requires a combination of emotions, positive thinking, and behavioural change from both parties.

Sometimes the husband might add verbal abuse to the injury of adultery, and this will hurt the wife even more than the adultery itself, especially if he compares her to his new love. Harsh words do go very deeply and create invisible wounds leaving scars that are hard to erase. If the husband continues having affairs, the woman becomes more dejected and the feelings of low self-esteem heighten.

Unquestionably, when low self-esteem exists in the marriage because of infidelity, it causes feelings of helplessness. This condition has a great influence on the already hurt woman if she constantly evaluates herself either with the husband's new lover or by the words he uses to describe her.

If a woman frequently hears negative statements from her husband, she spends more time thinking about what he said about her, rather than what he does. In the end, she begins to believe the negative things because she takes them seriously. I would consider low self-esteem an emotional tool, which manipulates an individual's thought pattern. It makes the individual believes things about the self that are not true.

Consequently, a combination of those destructive thoughts with the constant verbal abuses from her husband, only compound the situation as they all blend together to bring the wife under the subjection of low self-esteem.

Many couples will attest to the fact that often, the person they knew during the courtship, turned out to be a different person after the celebrations are over and the marriage begins. Being clad in the finest apparel, and the most expensive jewelries, do not make the ideal person for a monogamous lifetime relationship.

Sincere Love

To understand I Corinthians 13 is to view the prescriptive and absoluteness of love, and its necessity as an important component for successful marital interpersonal relationship. It is the understanding and application of this passage that will define the sincerity of one partner to the other because it is a responsibility that is shared by both husband and wife. In the discourse, Paul delineates a loving prescription for the partners as a protective device for maintaining the marital union.[12]

Love helps to form the foundation for securing stability within the marital relationship as is stated in the Scriptures. In the first place, Ephesians 5:25 identifies the husband as head of the wife, with instructions to love her even as Christ loves the church. This type of love is special and requires tenderness, understanding, forgiveness, and gentleness to maintain unity, which is vital to the relationship.

Secondly, the writer encouraged the wife to submit to her husband with sincerity and respect, and together their roles form the marital responsibility.

---

[12] "Love suffers long, and is kind; love envies not; love vaunteth not itself, is not puffed up. Doth not behave itself unseemly, seeks not her own, is not easily provoked, thinks no evil; rejoiced not in iniquity, but rejoices in the truth; bears all things, believeth all things, hopes all things, endures all things" (I Corinthians 13: 4-7).

Although I have only referred to love in a short space, no one needs to overstate what Paul has said in the love passage. Love is vital in any and every relationship, and each partner must treat the other similar to the way that person would like to be treated.

Moreover, there are different types of love, and not everyone expresses love the same way as another person does. For example, one person prefers gifts, while another likes touches and loving embraces. I do not believe that marital love needs any embellishment.

The Bible strictly says, "Love your wife" to the husband, and to the wife, "Submit to your husband." For more on love, go to[13]

---

[13] *"What is Love" Available* @ www.themarriagecorner.web.officelive.com

Chapter 10
Communication

According to Eisenman, "lack of communication in families does not necessarily mean that no one is talking."[14] It is true that even when a wife or husband does not say a word to each other, they are communicating. They communicate with body language, sighs, hums, attitudes, and so on. This "silent" style of communicating is common in all types of relationships.

Moreover, after a couple has lived together for a certain number of years, they learn each other's behaviours, peculiarities, and attitudes. Consequently, they each become respectful to their individual body language and even silent communication from each other. The husband is used to his wife's humming and knows if that is a signal to escape or draw near. The wife also, knows when to approach to ask for some extra cash, to report misbehaviour of the children, and so on.

Communication is vital in any and every relationship, but people will not always be talking with each other. Couples, who take time to communicate with each other in a loving way, will defeat the forces that will highjack their marriage.

Again, the couple will not always verbalize their feelings. They use smiles and warm touches to tell the other "I love you," no matter how long they have been married. Even children need to feel the warm touches of their parents.

Sadly, some parents do not hug their sons and daughters because they believe they are too old for such expressions. What parents fail to understand is that their children, despite how old they are, do need

---

[14] From T.L. Eisenman, *Temptations Families Face: Breaking Patterns That Keep Us Apart.* (InterVarsity Press, 1996), p.70ff.

warm touches that also say to them "I love you son, daughter." Furthermore, when there is warm communication in the home, this gives intruders a signal similar to that of a security system that sends off an alarm when they try to enter a building.

Likewise, when partners are communicating effectively, it means that there is a healthy family living inside that home and unwanted intruders will have difficulty gaining entrance. Evidently, a secure home where there are opportunities for open communication, laughter, expressions of love, joy, effective problem solving, and interaction will pose a threat to undesirable trespassers.

However, despite the fortresses of protection, the couple should always be on guard to prevent intrusions. One of the keys for maintaining an effective communication system is prayer. Although the family altar seems to have gone out of the home, it is time to bring it back to regain healthy family relationships. Prayer[15] has a tremendous impact in all of life's situations.

Unquestionably, effective communication is an essential component required in marriage because it forms the channel for a positive and enduring relationship. This means the interchange of opinions and ideas in conversations as each partner listens and pays attention to the other. There must be opportunity to reflect, clarify, ask questions, explain information, and express emotions.

Moreover, when partners are speaking, it is important to look the other in the eye because this shows that the person is attending. It shows interest and respect for the other.

Another way for communicating with each other is through body language, which gives an indication of whether the other person is listening, and if what is being conveyed is accepted or not. Body language will also indicate whether the speaker is congruent because that person might say one thing, but the body expresses something completely different.

---

[15] *"The Power of Prayer"* Available @ www.themarriagecorner.web.officelive.com

For instance, if one person is talking and the other ignores or looks bored, this sends a message that something is wrong because of the lack of interest. Besides, when partners do not communicate honestly with each other about what is happening in the relationship, they will make unilateral decisions based on misinterpretations and misperceptions that will invariably lead to a breakdown in the relationship.

There are times when the partners cease to communicate in a positive manner with each other, and a wide expanse of deep silence builds beams of stress and tension, even when they interact with each other. In those times, communication is a mixture of mumbles, sighs, shrugging of the shoulders, and silence; the demonstration of which is usually in anger.

According to Rabior & Leipert (1992), "anger has a spiral power in marriage. Its impact is largely negative and often highly destructive. It is the most potent marriage breaker of all," (p.10).

I would add that one of the behaviours that will spark anger is silence. Although there are no spoken words, the presence of silence will cause the other spouse to become angry. The reason is that silence will convey a greater meaning than words might do. Is it any wonder that 'silence' can be so hurtful?

Furthermore, it is our attitudes that tell the other person that we do not appreciate company or wish to enter into any dialogue. Regrettably, many times this lack of communication is caused by misinformation and misunderstandings.

Additionally, when someone has been hurt, that person may hold on to grudges and resentment that will affect the exchange of communication.

It is very important for the couple to communicate because it shows willingness to share hurts, misunderstandings, and mistakes, rather than pretend they do not exist. When partners discuss their problems together, this is an indication that there is an earnest desire to maintain a strong marital bond.

In addition, when God is in the marital relationship, there will be no holding on to hurts from one day to the next because the partners are careful not to let the enemy get a foothold in their lives.

Unfortunately, when problems of adultery occur, it seems easier for the innocent partner to point the finger at the adulterer while not admitting to his or her own contributions to the breakdown of the marriage. Facing up to faults and being open to communication will help to maintain a good interpersonal relationship.

While the couple will not escape problems because they are inherent in all types of relationships, they need to understand that communication will be the key factor for resolving the issues that cause the problems in the first place.

Surprisingly, but one of the partners might criticize, demean, and put down the other when there are problems. It seems that it is at such times that one of them uses the opportunity to throw insults towards the other. On another occasion that person would be careful and respectfully say things.

Therefore, the partners must deal with hurts and anger immediately, instead of waiting until when one person is upset because of misunderstandings. Furthermore, inconsistency and lack of congruency in communication will result in discord and turmoil.

Chapter 11

Maintaining Sexuality

One of the first signs of problems in some marriages is the absence of sexuality. Generally, this is due to the breakdown in communication between the partners because they are unwilling to admit to problems. Frequently, the relationship has deteriorated to a point where neither of the partners is speaking to the other. Well, if they are not talking, there is no love making either. It is only obvious that when the couple refuses to hold dialogues and converse with each other, neither will they want to share intimacy.

Invariably, when a wife finds out that her husband has been unfaithful, she locks down emotionally and does not want to have sex. She sees her husband as dirty, and for this reason she does not want to soil herself by associating with him, no matter how strong the desire. Women can be extremely strong when they plan to prove a point, even though this might mean sacrificing their own feelings.

Penny

When I discovered that Archie was seeing someone else, I did everything to get him out of our bed.

Phyllis

Every time he would turn to me, I would be snoring [pretending] or just give him the most of the bed. I did not want to have anything to do with him anymore.

Janice

There were times when I found all kinds of excuses to avoid having sex, especially when he had been away for days.

Although women will be distressed over their marital problems, this does not give them or their husband's permission to withhold sexual intimacy from each other if there is no evidence of adultery. I will not debate this because the Bible has its own answer:

> *Nevertheless, to avoid fornication, let every man have his own wife, and let every woman have her own husband. Let the husband render unto the wife due benevolence: and likewise also, the wife unto the husband. The wife hath not power of her own body, but the husband: and likewise also, the husband hath not power of his own body, but the wife. Defraud ye not one the other, except it be with consent for a time, that ye may give yourselves to fasting and prayer; and come together again, that Satan tempt you not for your incontinency (I Corinthians 7:2-5) KJV.*

If either of the partners disobeys this command, that person is guilty before God. A wife may ask, "What if my husband went and committed adultery. What should I do then?"

The biblical principles point out that it is God's will for the marriage to be healed because love and forgiveness can work together to restore the broken relationship. Consequently, the injured wife must be willing to forgive her husband if he acknowledges his fault and is willing to make a new start. Many marriages have improved after infidelity. However, there is no guarantee that every marriage will survive after infidelity, nor am I encouraging infidelity to strengthen a weak marriage. Positively, *no way* would I say this!

Although there are men who believe that having an *affair* outside of marriage will enrich the relationship, do not believe this myth. That is all it is, a myth. It is another one of Satan's schemes to put a wedge into the relationship. Besides, let every partner take note that with the incidences of diseases, the use of common sense and good judgment must precede resuming physical activities after an affair. It would therefore be sensible to seek medical advice to be on the safe side, and protect oneself.

If an adulterer became infected with any Sexually Transmitted Diseases, [STDs] he should get medical help before returning to his wife. She too, must be careful and not act impulsively. Women have developed all types of sexual diseases from their wandering husbands. *This is for both husband and wife to take heed!*

Still, the activity of sexuality in marriage does not mean dominance over each other, or outrageous sexual activities that are contrary to good Christian and moral principles. Each partner should learn how to please the other in decency and with respect within the context of spiritual wisdom, governed by common sense and what pleases the other person.

The fact that a couple has become one-flesh does not mean that one partner has the right to dictate personal preferences in order to dominate the other. Rather, the marital bed should have a sense of mutuality and order. God is everywhere and He sees everything [*See* Psalm 139].

Nevertheless, physical activity does not have to be the only form of sexuality between partners. It does not matter where they are, they can express themselves with devotion, tenderness, care, and love.

If the couple does not make every effort to keep love alive in the marriage by the demonstration of sexuality when they are together, the marriage will be heading for sure disaster because it will enter into a period of drought.

One of the reasons why many marriages fail is due to the lack of sexuality. Indeed, drought means dryness, fruitlessness, deadness, famine, and people end up starving and some even die. Similarly, a marriage that is not watered and fed with love and attention is no different from the dry desert. The desert does not bloom through lack of rain: and any marriage will become barren through sexual neglect and love.

Mistakenly, many couples believe that having sex is the only way of fulfilling sexuality in their relationship. Sex is neither the beginning nor the ending. Sex is only part of the devotion that leads to the ultimate. Think of marital sexuality as a full course meal with all the trimmings served in various places and on different platters and tablecloths.

Partners bear in mind, this menu is exclusive and very restrictive. Neither one of you should venture over into a strange person's plate, nor should you allow *anyone* else to share this platter. This is yours and yours solely!

Sometimes, take a romantic weekend somewhere just the two of you, especially after child rearing has ended. If the partners omit any or most of the items on the menu, after a while, life gets dull and becomes routine or stagnant.

Truly, without Christ and faith in the relationship, no marriage will survive. In addition, every couple must recognize that after the wedding and festivities are over, each of them has a life to live together.

Nevertheless, the partners will need guidance, and it would be advisable to seek out some type of marital counseling before the wedding, and for the first six months.

In addition, associating with mature couples who have successfully overcome many disasters and hurdles in their marriage, would be ideal from whom to gain help and advice, rather than from inexperienced persons.

Chapter 12

Factors That Influence Marriage

Many situations will influence a marriage that will change its structure and the relationship of the partners. Most of those factors are to be found in the social milieu of society, while others are personal differences. This chapter highlights the most prominent ones.

The Sexual Explosion

From around the time of the sixties, the world has seen a moral decline with an increased and insatiable craving for sex, and more sex. Illicit sex has become the world's most social explosive device that has destroyed many marriages and lives.

Sex has been made so glamorous that it is now found in three types of wrappers: physical sex, telephone sex, and cyberspace sex. Included in this arrangement is the same-sex mind-set.

In order for the purveyors of this commodity to reach their clients, almost every billboard is displayed with some hint of sexual expression. Cars are sold with sex; food is sold with sex. People have become so preoccupied and obsessed with sex that it has taken over the theme of nearly all television programs, musicals and dramas; and with all types of implements to influence the onlooker or listener.

The expressions of sex have even overshadowed some of the so-called gospel programs by the types of costumes/dress of the so-called "spiritual" performers.

Magazines, articles, dress, even the way some people talk and walk; one can find some trace of sexual enticement. The programs in the media are saturated with this unquenchable desire to bombard the audience with some kind of sexual article of trade. This sexual revolution has brought it to the forefront of all other interests.

The obsessive interest in sex occupies the lives of people, and extends from the political arena to the pulpit of church leaders. Admittedly, sex of itself is not sinful. What makes sex sinful is the immorality attached to this God-given means for marital happiness. Biblically, the activity was reserved for marriage. However, since the Fall sex has evolved with many skews regarding its pleasure and use, thus distorting its intended purpose.

Moreover, for many years the concept of "sex" was considered to be one of those words that were used with a hush and whisper in public, and only in certain environments. However, today the assumption is that from the age of puberty or before, children are now more aware of what sex is, and they can give graphic explanations of the sexual act. There was a time when children were allowed to grow up.

Unfortunately, parents have allowed the media to dictate the nurturing and development of their children. This has revolutionized the concept of marriage, family, and relationships. Each day one can view, hear, or read about episodes of immoral behaviours across boundaries that were once kept free from such assault on the lives of individuals. Mistakenly, this presentation of immorality is seen as "free speech" from the stages of the arts.

Clearly, if such immoral cultures are allowed to permeate the society unchecked, the implication is that it might eventually become the standard for moral values; and the clean, safe, and pure values of Christianity will be muted into obscurity.

Sex has been glorified, magnified, and almost deified by those who believe there can be no other means of pleasure to cure their insatiable addictive appetites. Occasionally, one hears of individuals who will admit that they cannot be content with only one person for a continued monogamous relationship.

Additionally, the sexual explosion has inflated two despicable predators: incest, and rape. They are indeed predators because the perpetrators behave like looters with their victims. They steal their identity, and self-confidence, as they ravage their innocence, and dignity. Those victims end up with invisible emotional wounds that leave scars, which they bury deeply in the recesses of their minds. Eventually the pain from those wounds may continue throughout life.

Incest

The incidence of incest has become one of the most repulsive behaviours for anyone who has endured this horrible experience. What makes it so dreadful is that in some homes, the incident is evident, but mothers, fearful of their husband or boyfriend's behaviour will turn a blind eye and a deaf ear to their children's cry for help.

In a marital relationship, the memory of incest is one of those situations that might make a woman see adultery as tolerable because she fears having to expose herself sexually to another man. The memories of the past become a fortress that keeps her imprisoned as she remains with her husband despite his insensitive behaviours. She seems to accept the old adage, "better the devil you know than the one you do not know."

Admittedly, the occurrence of childhood molestation is not new, but it seems to have become quite prevalent from the uncontrolled desires relating to the sexual explosion in society. This crime against children is an evil that has emerged as an integral item on the social menu of immoral behaviours.

Seemingly, since "sin" is hardly referred to even in many pulpits, individuals who are caught up in immorality may think that no one is being hurt by their behaviours. Unmistakably, if church leaders are not speaking out against the sinful nature of humans, then certain immoral acts will be overlooked.

Then again, with the new "rights" that are generating daily, many leaders will be muzzled to avoid legal repercussions. Indeed, we have reached an age where sin has become attractive. Therefore, most behaviours once deemed immoral, are now being accepted with open arms in society. Christians are admonished to be the lights of the world and salt of the Earth. However, if religious leaders are ignoring the evidence of sin, this leaves the door of immorality wide open to the world.

Rape

Rape is another sexual predator to invade even marriages. I pause here to say that while many incidents are indeed rape, there are times when a woman on a date entices a man with flirtatious behaviours. The man in turn, voluntarily accepts her encouragement as an invitation for sex. Whilst in the midst of play, the woman may decide that she will turn off her romantic switch; but the man, due to his masculine nature is unable to do so as quickly as she can.

The caution here is for women to take heed concerning the types of *signals* they display when they are alone with the opposite sex. We have all heard that if you play with fire, it will burn you. Nevertheless, this does not give *any* man the right to humble a woman. *Any* form of rape is still *very* wrong.

I now turn to the horrible case of rape. It is unimaginable to understand the fear and anguish an individual goes through to be taken against his or her will to fulfill a sexual act. This occurs both in and out of marriage; and with children, both boys and girls alike.

Rape is one of the most shameful sexual behaviours that humanity has known. Although some perpetrators may feel remorse and regret for their actions, there are those who blame the woman, thus adding more pain to her already injured emotions.

Nevertheless, there are a few men who were found guilty of this dreadful crime, and who have confessed that they were better off left in prison because they cannot help themselves. Others have even requested to have their instruments removed.

It does not matter what the treatment or sentence is for the perpetrators, the fact remains that the experience leaves wounds with invisible emotional scars, and longstanding outcomes for the victims who have experienced rape. The trauma and memories can even serve as a lifetime punishment when that rape produces a child.

Moreover, the rape victim usually carries memories that can lock the individual into a prison from which there seems to be no reparation or escape. What recompense can there be for one who was taken with such force and indecency?

Continues in the next chapter

Chapter 13

Factors That Influence Marriage

[Part 2]

Married women who have suffered the indignity and humiliation of rape in their childhood are sometimes very unresponsive to their husbands each time the memory returns. Some women will go through the sexual act as a form of duty with no pleasure or interest.[16]

Obviously, a husband who is aware of his wife's unresponsiveness may tolerate this for a while, but later he may decide that he can receive satisfaction and enjoyment outside of the marriage.

Other husbands are supportive, and they will encourage their wives to seek help to improve the relationship. Still, in some cases, the wife is in denial and is unwilling to admit that she needs help.

There should be no disgrace conveyed to a rape victim. Nevertheless, when rape has been proven with certainty, initially the woman is invariably taken to shreds on the judicial platform of the courts. Lawyers for the defense usually make every effort to prove the alleged perpetrator innocent of this abominable crime.

In contrast, the victim is made to re-live the experience, and all personal past histories of sexual activities are exhumed so that she is put on trial before the public.

What could be worse than for the rape victim to be paraded before millions as the instigator of a crime for which she has suffered, while a lawyer coaches the perpetrator how to behave in court?

---

[16] D.A. Seamands *Healing of Emotions,* "Unhealed sexual traumas carried into married life often produce a terrible inner conflict of wanting sex but hating it at the same time". In *Healing Your Hearts of Painful Emotions*, (Inspiration Press, NY, 1993), p.360.

Some of those men have all types of excuses such as; *I did not know what I was doing. I was drunk. I thought she was my wife. She wanted it...*

Eventually, those rapists who escape punishment by the skillfulness of their lawyers will create a principle for the disproportion of justice, and double jeopardy will be issued to the victim who has suffered shame and humiliation at the hands of someone who could not control his or her sexual passions. I say his or her because women too have been known to commit rape and incest.

By double jeopardy, I mean that the woman suffered the experience of the crime; also the humiliation from the perpetrator's lawyer, and still worse if she was impregnated or if the perpetrator was acquitted.

Understandably, lawyers are there to seek justice for a defendant; but if the evidences are beyond doubt, why put the woman on trial. Furthermore, the victim has to carry that emotional pain and scar which can be a life-long experience, maybe from childhood into adulthood.

Additionally, if a victim of rape enters marriage with this memory and later has to face infidelity, the emotional pain will be exceeded, as the trauma becomes more permanent.

A woman in this situation can become indifferent to the adulteries of her husband. This is especially so if the children have grown, and she has other interests that will fulfill the loneliness and shame of her husband's inconsistencies.

Moreover, if the rape victim did not report the incident, obviously that individual received no support after the experience. The result is that the memories will become the deciding factor in future relationships.

Further, the memory of the event can become a defense mechanism against both surface and deep relationships. Some victims build up a hatred for the opposite sex. Others may have fears about sex that keep them in bondage.

I must mention here that some married women experience rape from their husbands. Sometimes this happens because the husband is drunk, or maybe the woman was just not in the mood to reciprocate his advances.

Another reason why she would not be aroused could be due to adulteries or physical abuse received from the husband. These are reasons why a wife might refuse to have sex, and the husband would force her to respond to his demands whether she is willing or not.

Parental Rejection

Rejection is not a situation that many people are capable of dealing with at any time of life. It is a negative emotion, which leaves scars throughout the life of the individual. Moreover, the memory will affect the marital relationship because it is an unhealthy emotion.

Parental rejection lasts longer than most other situations a child will encounter. The reason is that the emotion of rejection can be considered as the refusal to acknowledge that child as a person who needs love, nurture, and attention. It gets even worse when that child is made to feel inferior to other siblings. It is discouraging, and if the situation is not dealt with or resolved early in life, the individual may take that feeling into a marital relationship.

Furthermore, if that relationship turns out to be an unfaithful marital situation, this will ignite the past hurts of rejection and make the woman feel disappointment with herself, or even life. It is very difficult for someone who has faced parental rejection to deal with marital rejection successfully without professional intervention, and the help of God's Holy Spirit. Besides, parental rejection has been considered one of "the most painful kinds of rejections..."[17]

---

[17] From D.A. Seamands, *Healing of Memories*: "The most painful kinds of rejection occur during the earliest years of life – preschool and the early grades – because there is no way of explaining the reason for an action which infants or children interpret as rejection." In *Healing Your Hearts of Painful Emotions*, (Inspirational Press, NY, 1993): p.299.

Pride and Self-centeredness

Self-centeredness is an ego birthed from pride. It is a narcissistic view of the self that makes the individual thinks that he or she is better than anyone else is. If a spouse believes he or she is better for reasons such as educational ability or economic status, this will affect the quality of the relationship and threaten the life of the marriage. Pride is one of those deadly sins to have infiltrated the behaviours of humanity.

Furthermore, we cannot fail to observe that it was pride, which caused the devil his place in Heaven. Therefore, he knows the influence of this evil that often destroys morals, relationships, and families. Nonetheless, people are not usually aware of the influence of pride. The Bible states: "*Pride goeth before destruction, and a haughty spirit before a fall*" (Proverbs 16:18).

Apparently, the sequence of pride is *self-centeredness, ego, idolatry, destruction*, leading to *separation* from God. Still, while people are alive because of Jesus' death, burial, and resurrection there is hope if they repent. To repent means to turn away from sin. I have listened to arguments that Jesus did not turn away anyone who came to him. What those persons fail to understand is that, while Jesus did not turn away the sinner, he often tells them "go, and sin no more."

Common-Law Constructs

In addition, another social construct threatening marriage that has become acceptable and institutionalized, is the common-law arrangement. In this setting, a couple lives as man and wife although they have not gone through a marriage ceremony. It is true that God seems to have winked over this arrangement, but it is still wrong.

For some persons this partnership is a form of trial marriage to see if the two are compatible with each other. Some people have lived in this set-up for over many decades, and still cannot decide whether they love each other to make a firm commitment.

Children have been born out of this formation, and did not know that parents were not married to each other. Christian singles need not follow this principle because they have the privilege to approach God to seek His guidance on every aspect concerning His plan for their life. Asking God to choose a partner is sufficient, and waiting on His direction is a test of faith and trust in His wisdom.

Unusual Factors

Even in the Christian marriage, there are situations when a partner may have had unfulfilled sexual expectancies carried over into the relationship. Others may have personal desires that were hidden, such as sexual orientation and over-attraction to the opposite sex or same gender preferences.

Such persons may have been under the misguided belief that married life would change those desires. Suddenly, they find themselves plunged into sinful acts that will result into problems, and in some cases, the demise of the marriage.

Therefore, pre-marital preparation and knowing each other's innate temperament are vital for a long marital relationship. This does not mean that deception is inevitable all the way. The reason is that there may be fear of revealing one's likes and dislikes making an individual keep them under cover.

Apparently, marriage will not *always* change a person's behaviour. However, when those surprises emerge, both persons need to seek for outside help to resolve the situation. Failure to acknowledge and deal with problems, only make matters worse.

Chapter 14

The Future of Marriage

On another note, with the invasion of same-sex marriages, I ask the following questions: Where is marriage going? What does the future holds for marriage? The universal belief was that marriage was between one man and one woman. Unfortunately, today we are hearing of same-sex marriages. What makes matters worse is that the thrust for alternative life-style has penetrated the church community.

Moreover, proponents for this belief are assiduously campaigning for more rights, despite the fact that those beliefs are contrary to the Word of God.

The implication is that if the church sits back and takes comfort in a comatose state while morals continue to decline even in its midst, it seems that the Christian marriage will no longer take centre stage in the lives of most men and women. It is clear to see that societal desires have unleashed a deathblow on marriage as new concepts are birthed from the womb of theorists' ideologies. Seemingly, man is still asking the question, "Did God say one man and one woman, and together they make one-flesh?"

However, while God's Word does not change, there are people who will negate the meaning of marriage that is set by God in order to satisfy their desires; if only to impose their defiance, and own interpretations.

With the foregoing, it would seem that the biblical model for marriage is eroding. Nonetheless, only those who have chosen another pattern would accept this idea. Furthermore, if marriage is dying, those women who have remained in unfaithful relationships are doing so at a great risk. One reason why marriage would seem to be dying is that "the substitution of cohabitation for marriage would result in lower overall rates of marriage for the less religious" (*See* Thornton, Axinn & Hill 1992).

The assumption is that people's attitude towards religion and morals seem to guide them in their concept to the importance of marriage. In contrast, another report stated that cultural, demographic, economic, and social sources have produced a transformation in the institution of marriage over the past century (Furstenberg, 1990).

On a more hopeful note, despite the increase in the rate of divorces, people are still getting married. Some of them are doing so for the right reasons and in the right way, while others are following their hedonistic ways to gratify their own desires.

The New Sex Craze
One novelty affecting the biblical model for marriage is the explosion of cyberspace romance where partners are having electronic sexual affairs. This is indeed a scheme from the pit of hell. Included in this sex craze is telephone sex.

These are typical devices to destroy *all* marriages. Evidently, if marriages are destroyed by the infectious social diseases of immorality, then the family system will be affected. Undoubtedly, if the structure of marriage continues on this downward spiral, then the next generation is in serious moral and spiritual danger.

The question proposed here: "Is there a difference between cyberspace, telephone, and physical sex?" From the biblical perspective there is no difference because Jesus taught that the very *thought* of having sexual desires outside of marriage is evidence of adultery.

How easy it would be to say, "But we have *never* had sex, we only *talked* sex talk." Every action starts with a thought, which, if left ungoverned, will occasionally thrive into a full-grown act. The enemy begins in the mind (*See* Proverbs 4:23), which is his greatest battlefield for the human race.

Moreover, Christians must be careful not to follow the world's ideology of changing partners because this behaviour makes them live beneath their godly privileges, and weakens their spiritual values. Furthermore, the world cannot teach a godly person how to maintain sanctity in marriage with ideas from the evil kingdom of darkness.

Those standards are for the woman to have power to do what *she* wants, when *she* wants, and if *she* wants because she is not being led or controlled by the Holy Spirit. This type of ideology is unbiblical. Obviously, the modern interpretation of marriage is usually against what God ordained marriage to be. Christian spouses must be very careful to walk according to God's will so that they do not fall into the mire of inconsistencies.

Worldly Ideals

Although marriages are susceptible to problems, divorce is not always the remedy for marital problems, because in the first place, it is contrary to what God intended for marriage. In any case, how can someone pour petrol onto a fire that has already been lit? Secondly, to offer the advice of divorce to a couple whose marriage is in danger of crashing in order to seek freedom is not the solution to healing of the problems.

When Paul admonished husbands to love their wives, he used Jesus' love for the church as an analogy to crystallize what he meant (*See* Ephesians 5:25). This teaching is not an error in the Bible. It is God's truth! Infidelity is sinful and will forever be so because God's Word will never change to suit the ideals and passions of those who are defiant to His laws.

Besides, if the world sets a standard for the sanctity of marriage that is contrary to God's plan, then Christian couples ought not to conform to those standards that will nullify the sacredness of marriage, corrupt their beliefs, and jeopardize their walk with God. The world's standard appears to have the tune of *"let's love and get married today; if it does not work out, let's get divorced tomorrow."*

It would appear to be similar to what took place in the days of Moses when husbands would divorce their wives if they accidentally burned the food. It did not take much for a man to obtain a divorce in those days, and so it is today.

Marriage will remain Unchanged

Despite the changes to the institution of marriage, the Christian perspective on marriage has remained intact since God joined the first couple in a one-flesh union. God was against adultery then, and still is, even in this millennium. God considers marriage to be permanent, and only death should bring about any separation.

Despite the changes and some peoples' ideas about marriage, others reverence God's Word; and are still holding to the principles for the Christian model. Those standards will remain until Jesus returns.

Additionally, although there are those who give the biblical model a low grade, it is still the greatest social partnership humanity has ever known. It surpasses all other relationships. Therefore, this type of marriage requires careful thought before anyone enters into this sacred union.[18]

Nevertheless, the Christian marriage will continue to be part of the family system, but there is a strong competition with this model and the new same-sex model that is being thrust into the framework.

What other ideas will emerge in an attempt to destroy the Christian marriage – God's plan for marriage? I have no answers.

---

[18] *"TEN Questions to ask myself before I say I DO"* Available @ www.themarriagecorner.web.officelive.com

Chapter 15

Same-sex Marriages

Marriages of today are not lasting and there has to be a reason for this situation. Could it be that many people have changed the glory of the Christian marriage into their own hedonistic image?

The Bible teaches that each man should have his own wife. It also teaches that from the beginning of time God made male and female, and they were joined into one flesh making them a unit in essence. This is not my idea; it came from the Holy Bible that has been around for many centuries, the contexts from which many social and moral laws were set.

However, with what seems to be a new morality, and what appears to be a new translation of the Bible, the same-gender partnership is challenging the concept of the male-female marriage. Even members of the clergy are opting for same-sex partnership. Does this mean that the Bible is wrong? *No! Never!*

Let me interject here that God is totally and utterly against any *behaviour* that is contrary to His Word. He loves the sinner, but hates the sin. Furthermore, the Blood of Jesus Christ and his love can change the vilest sinner if that person willingly repents. I will quickly add that I am against *any* act of violence towards *any* person because of a religious belief, or personal orientation.

The mission of the believer in Christ is to see that the sinner repents and turns to Christ with a true heart. Love covers a multitude of sin, and while we may abhor ungodly behaviours, it is our duty as Christians to win each person with love. Harbouring hatred for any one is against God's will because He loved us even while we were yet sinners.

Although, there are those who will turn a blind eye and a deaf ear to the moral decay in society with the resulting destruction of the Christian marriage, God's Word will remain unchanged. Moreover, empirical research or humanistic arguments can *never* prove that since creation God made a mistake concerning the structure of marriage, never!

The Bible clearly declares, male and female made He. That is, Adam and Eve, and *no other arrangement.* Still, God made us with wills to choose, both morally and spiritually. If anyone decides not to follow the teachings of the Bible it is his or her choice, and not because God made a mistake.

Clearly, the concept of same-sex marriage may be accepted by the world's standard, but from the biblical perspective, this partnership was never within God's plan for marital relationship, and He will turn away from the rebellious (*See* Romans 1).

It is sad to note that people in high places are allowing political and societal persuasions to govern their decisions regarding truth and morality, rather than by what they know to be right. We could ask who is the real enemy in all of this. The Bible states: *"For we wrestle not against flesh and blood, but against principalities, against powers, against the rulers of spiritual wickedness in high places."*[19]

As Christians, we have a spiritual obligation to be forgiving and loving toward those whose eyes have become dimmed, and ears hardened to the precepts that have been laid down for godly and moral living.

While we are deeply grieved when we see the disobedience and defiance towards both natural and biblical laws, we cannot put ourselves in the place of God to annihilate or even to call down fire to

---

[19] Ephesians 6:12.

consume the perpetrators of evil. Jesus came to save *all* sinners, and that was the reason why He shed his Blood on Calvary's Cross.

Admittedly, in biblical times the person who sinned according to the behaviours of Sodom and Gomorrah [S&G] would have been destroyed by God's wrath. Let me pause here. Very often, people only think about the result of [S&G]. Just hearing the names seems to conjure up thoughts in their minds. However, what brought their destruction was their *pride* coupled with their *defiant* behaviours.[20]

When people disobey God because they think themselves better and wiser than He is, then He will show them who is in control of this world. *God made this world all by Himself, and He can destroy it if He wills. It is His world.*[21] I firmly believe that the time will come when God will say, "enough is enough, and it is time for action."

Let us get this straight, it is irrelevant whether some people believe in the reality of God or do not. When God is ready, there will be no man-made laws, or personal preferences that will be able to stop Him. For that reason, those of us who trust in God and obey His Word, let us not allow the depraved habits of humanity to weaken our faith in Him. God will not fail and He does not change. Therefore, let us wait and see what He will do in His time.

Undoubtedly, the presence of same-sex marriage/partnership has threatened the Christian marriage so that it seems to nullify God's intention for marriage. The new model is an absolute disrespect for God's plan concerning marriage, family, and procreation, and an obvious disobedience of His Laws.

Frankly, no one can force another person to choose the way he or she wants to go. Evidently, sentence must be left up to God to deal with perpetrators and proponents for their ungodly behaviours and attitudes against His Laws. This includes all manner of evils.

---

[20] Ezekiel 16:49, Romans 1:21-26ff
[21] Psalm 24

On another note, many Christians only point out unnatural and *certain* behaviours to be abominations. Nevertheless, there are other abominable sins, which they fail to note. One of such sins is lying (Proverbs 6:17). We cannot hide the fact that many liars are in churches, who are robed in clerical garb, and some who march up in the choir loft every Sunday.

Including are those who teach Sunday School, play the organ and piano, dance, and raise their hands just like any other *holy* woman or man of God. Yet, God has not destroyed them because He is forgiving, loving, merciful, and longsuffering.[22]

We must be careful not to take judgment away from God because it is of His mercies that we are not *all* destroyed.

God hates *all* manner of sins, and I do not think there is any sin more tolerant to God than another would be.

---

[22] II Peter 3:9

Chapter 16

Preserving the Relationship

Although the Bible sets precise standards for marriage, Christian marriages are just as vulnerable for interpersonal disputes, adulteries, and divorces as any other.

Some researchers are of the opinion that those marriages are failing at a rate that is just as great as non-Christians. This may sound alarming, but any marriage will fail if the couple does not have a solid relationship with the Lord.

Any marriage has a chance of surviving if both partners spend time with the Lord so that he can impart grace, strength, and courage for the awesome task as parents, and as partners.

Besides, marriages will fail if the couple does not adhere to the basic principles of love, commitment, loyalty, and forgiveness. This means that each partner must hold fast to the Word of God and not conform to world standards because this will cause marital shipwreck.

Moreover, when problems develop in the marriage, it is not always that the partners will immediately opt for divorce. They may decide to keep the marriage intact, but they may only co-exist as a couple going through the routine, while presenting a charade to the world. In some cases, members of the family are not aware of the problems the couple is facing in the marriage.

However, it is not only the desire to keep one's marriage intact that will prevent disaster, but learning how to maintain the principles by which all marriages should be governed.

Those principles include forgiveness, truthfulness, commitment, honesty, faithfulness, respect, trust, kindness, and love among others.

These are fundamental for the stability and permanence of marriage. These are what help to preserve the life and quality of the relationship.

Spiritual Abuse

The desire of every Christian couple is for the entire family to know Jesus Christ in a personal way. In addition, the situation where only one partner is a Christian, there is the wish to have the other person adhere to Christian principles. For example, when a wife is the only one professing Christianity, she will work ardently to get her husband to change into a saintly garment, which he will stubbornly refuse to do.

Some wives are so passionate with "religion" that when they are fasting everyone else in the home must also be on fast by making unilateral decisions without input from the husband. This is more evident when the wife became a Christian after marriage. This behaviour will affect the relationship and cause constant quarrels, and in some cases result in abuses.

The presence of spiritual abuse in the home refers to forcing one's religious principles on children and a spouse in a domineering and controlling manner.[23]

Let me say, that it does not matter how loudly or how often a Christian wife plays religious CDs and tapes in an attempt to force a partner or children to serve the Lord, those types of behaviours will only cause strife in the home, and will hurt the relationship. No one can change the sinner. God is the only person who has that power because conviction comes through the Holy Spirit, rather than intimidation and control.

It is important to note that the devil is subtle, and he knows how to use a good thing and make it bad. Therefore, witnessing requires wisdom, and commonsense. Besides, the most effective witnessing in the home is by example and not verbal insults and accusations.[24] Spiritual abuse will certainly lead to other kinds of manipulations that

---

[23] *See* Matthew 23:1-8; Mark 7:1-16.
[24] Colossians 4:6

will wreck the relationship and even completely disintegrate it if the marriage ends in divorce.

Physical Changes

Another important matter of significance is the occurrence of the physical changes and life events that will take place. These life transitions can make a big difference in the relationship, both physically and emotionally. Being a Christian does not stop those changes from taking place.

The Bible teaches: "*Where there is no vision, the people perish.*[25]" This same principle also applies to marriage. Both husband and wife ought to keep themselves informed on the physical developmental changes that might affect their relationship as they mature in age. The fact that the partners have a strong Christian marriage will not exclude them from the vicissitudes of life.

Two of those events that will take place are menopause and mid-life crises. They are transitional developmental stages in life that can cause severe damages to the relationship if either of the partners does not know the signs and symptoms of such events.

The changes are physical life-changing events similar to the way our hair gets gray. We grow older every day and our bodies change. Therefore, it is imperative that each person is aware and pays attention to the changes that will take place.

For this reason, keeping up with regular medical examinations would be very helpful, along with informative literature, and attending workshops and seminars on important topics relating to life's changes. These help us to see that developmental changes are normal events in our lives.

Prayer alone will not work in some cases. Moreover, God gave doctors understanding and wisdom about the human body, and they use this knowledge to help us to take care of ourselves.

---

[25] Proverbs 29:18a.

If partners are aware and cognizant of the physical life changes that will occur, they will be more prepared to meet those symptoms comfortably, instead of being taken by surprise.

For instance, I do not believe that a usually pleasant woman in her fifties suddenly decides on an impulse to be nagging and irritable. There must be some hormonal, physiological, psychological, or emotional reasons. In fact, one could even infer that the inter-relatedness of those factors may be the cause for changes in the woman's behaviour.

Likewise, a man who suddenly decides to get involved in an extramarital relationship may not do it out of mere casual curiosity, especially if he had been faithful throughout the relationship. I am not here to minimize the mistakes partners make in a marriage. Instead, I am trying to reveal some of the situations that partners will face in the marriage.

Often wives put all their marital problems on the devil or someone else. They blame the other woman, the mother-in-law and just about anyone who can sustain the weight of their diatribes.

While outsiders are frequently contributory to the marital disputes, if spouses would take inventory of themselves, their own weaknesses and faults; then they would not cast *all* the blame on others or even their husbands.

It takes two to build a marriage. Therefore, it takes two to break the relationship. Every couple should maintain a balance in securing the relationship.

The responsibility does not rest on only one person. They must work in unison with God's help to keep the life of the marriage until such time that they part.

Chapter 17

Marriage Requires Hard Work

Some Christians have a way of adopting the ostrich-style behaviour by burying their heads in prayer with a "let the Lord handle it" type of composure. The Lord will handle it.

However, there are times when individuals have to do some things for themselves that the Lord will not do for them. Naturally, without knowledge and understanding, a marriage will begin to decay as neglect sets in. The relationship will dissipate into nothingness, and only an imitation will remain.

Lest the reader should think that I live in an ideal Christian society where everything is heavenly, I must emphasize that *not all Christian marriages are secure.*

There is a real devil who acts as an instigator and who hates to see a good relationship thrives. While it is better for both partners to be born again and living for the Lord, there is no guarantee that *all* will go well in the marriage.

Undeniably, marriages, even the Christian ones, mean hard work for both partners. *Prayer alone will not work.* Therefore, Christian partners must make every effort to tend to the marriage as a gardener takes care of his garden. God has set up a plan for marriage.

Nevertheless, Christian marriages as all others need constant maintenance of devotion and care from each partner to the other in order to keep it beautiful, attractive, and enticing.

Setting your Priorities

One of the weaknesses that cause Christian marriages to fail is because there are wives who leave their husbands at home while they go out with their friends. They will attend every service; and are involved with every ministry with very little time to spend with their husbands, and children. These are *holy women* of God, who believe that their ministries must come before their families.

Those women are driven by their ministerial egos, and guided by their adult-juvenile mentalities. They are the ones who will be asking for prayer for their husbands when the man has taken all that he can and decides to take action. Do not get me wrong; I am not in favour for the breakup of a marriage whatever the cause.

Rather, my intention is to provoke those women to look at their priorities, their duties as Christian wives, and God's plan for marriage. More than once the admonition to the wife is submissiveness (*See* Colossians 1:18 & Ephesians 5:22).

Obviously, those wives, though Christians, have adopted the worldly standards of doing what they want, when they want; whilst their husbands wait in line until they are ready to behave like dutiful wives.

Sadly, for many, that time often comes *much* too late. Today they are reaping the whirlwind from sowing to the wind in their passion for self-gratification from their ministries. Your family comes first, and before your ministry.

Wives who refuse to submit to their husbands in carrying out their duties will certainly pay the price. Those types of behaviours make it difficult for the world to understand the Christian marriage other than that it is a covenant relationship.

If the Christian wife believes this fact, then what is she doing to demonstrate this to the world? The Bible teaches *"Be not conformed to this world: but be ye transformed by the renewing of your mind..."* (Romans 12:2a). Clearly, if the Christian wife does not live up to the will of the Lord concerning marriage and submissiveness, she is in total disobedience to his desires for marriage.

Respect

I have seen women return a disdainful look towards their husbands. I just chuckle when I see them. If a woman is not satisfied with her husband's behaviour, it is her duty to tell him in private. When wives treat their husbands with coldness because of ignorance, that man might accept the behaviour for a while.

However, his seemingly compliance might just be the opportunity he was waiting for to wander from the relationship. Remember, *"Where there is no vision the people perish."*[26] This is *your* marriage, and it takes both of you to build a successful relationship.

Besides, adulterers rarely ever go for less or worse; it is always more or better! Let us face it, invariably a sixty-year old man will find himself a pretty young thing [PTY], who is attractive and delightful.

Very rarely will that man become interested in a woman his age. Usually, those men seek for warm romantic adventures; physical excitement; passionate love; tender friendship; and affectionate enticement; which some wives fail to give.

Every man likes to look at an attractive woman, but some women have lived so long with an unforgiving spirit, so that they no longer know how to be soft and tender even to the touch of their husbands. If you ask me, they are romantically dead, and they are the ones guilty of killing their marriage.

Women have killed their marriages by showing disdain and rudeness, especially when the man is not one who will respond in like manner. There are good men who have been trodden under by women who do not respect them. Each partner should respect, and care for each in order to maintain effective communication and prevent incidences of bickering and fights.

Leaders must Delegate

Still, I must be fair because one of the major failures with many leaders is that they do not delegate. They spend more time with their ministries

---

[26] Proverbs 29:18

than they do at home. With some ministers, it is always the next revival; the next conference; the next service; the next funeral; and the next, and the next until suddenly the children are all grown and they do not know them.

Their wives grow away from them and romance becomes dull or non-existent. It is time for Christians to get wise and take care of their families as they do their ministries.

Even if you are a pastor or leader, your family comes before your ministry. The Bible states that if you cannot rule your own homes successfully, then you are not fit to be a leader (*See* I Timothy 3:2-4; Titus 1:6-9).

I repeat, after God your family comes before your ministry. Moreover, when leaders do not take care of their children and spend time with them, they are disobeying God's Word (*See* Ephesians 6:4; Colossians 3:21). Children need their parents. Furthermore, fathers have the mandate to lead the home. If they are not present, the wife is left to manage, nurture, discipline, and do a million and one things, all by herself.

Leaders must delegate to reliable workers in the ministry so that they can take time for rest and with their family. Moreover, one of the principles of effective leadership is being able to delegate.

Take an example from Moses. When Jethro, his father-in-law saw how he spent the entire day taking all the complaints from the people, he said to Moses

"The thing that thou doest is not good. Thou wilt surely wear away, both thou, and this people that is with thee: for this thing is too heavy for thee; thou art not able to perform it thyself alone. So Moses hearkened to the voice of his father-in-law, and did all that he had said" (Exodus 18:17b-18, 24).

Consequently, if delegating was good for Moses, why take on more than you can bear. Think about it.

Family Night

Leaders should reserve at least one night each week when the phone is off. This is the time for family conferences, family discussions, and so on. Those times are significant opportunities where each member of the family can express, while the others listen. It is true that we live in a very busy, microwave age; but this must not stop the opportunities for family dialogue.

There must be some time during the seven-day week when the family can get together. This is even more vital when the children are young. They need help so that they do not go astray. It does not make sense waiting until the horse is out the gate to shut it. It will be too late then!

Re-kindle the Fire

It does not matter what the age is, both partners must take time out for each other. Sometimes go out and re-kindle that fire that has burnt to ash. It only takes a spark to get that fire going again.

Well, trying to get a blaze might make smoke that will get into your eyes; but keep at it, be persistent, and the flames will eventually come. The point is, *get with it – together* - as much, and as often as you can!

Alternatively, if you wish to remain at home: light a candle and set the tone, to enhance that relationship. Every marriage needs loving attraction, spicy enticement, enrichment, and romance!

These come from both partners in the relationship, and not from the outside. Because you are Christians does not mean you are too old to love each other. A touch of paint can make even an old building looks good.

PART II
Marital Unfaithfulness

Can a man take fire in his bosom, and his clothes not be burned? Can one go upon hot coals, and his feet not be burned? So he that goes in to his neighbour's wife; whosoever touches her shall not be innocent (Proverbs 6: 27-29) KJV.
But whoso commits adultery with a woman lacks understanding: he that doeth it destroys his own soul (Proverbs 6:32) KJV.
For this cause shall a man leave father and mother, and shall cleave to his wife: and they twain shall be one flesh. Moses because of the hardness of your hearts suffered you to put away your wives: but from the beginning it was not so (Matthew 19:5, 8)

The Section covers the following:

- The Biblical View of Infidelity
- Sexual Purity in Marriage
- It is a Social Germ
- Some Reasons for Infidelity
- Myths About Infidelity
- The Charade
- Why Men Cheat
- Why Women in Unfaithfulness

Chapter 18

The Biblical View of Infidelity

"But I say unto you, That whosoever looks on a woman to lust after her hath committed adultery with her already in his heart" (Matthew 5:28).

According to the Bible, when a man goes to a strange woman it is like taking fire into his bosom.[27] It is therefore hard to imagine that an adulterer does not feel the fire of shame, remorse, and regret, knowing he has violated his wife, and that he could bring diseases to her. Infidelity is an unconscionable selfish behaviour because of the thoughtlessness of the person who is caught up in its grip.

Despite the health dangers attached to this behaviour, infidelity has become very common just about everywhere from the highest to the lowest in all areas of life. It has no respect of persons, whether saint or sinner adultery will come knocking on the door looking for an entrance.

Furthermore, the prevalence of extra-marital behaviours has become so tolerable an occurrence, so that it has changed the definition of marriage. The result is that adultery has become an acceptable norm in society, without caution or restraint.

What is even worse is that, once this social virus infects the marriage, the entire family suffers. This suffering continues through the years, especially if there are children involved.

For example, in some cases divorce filters down into the next generation. It is time for the world to understand that the behaviour of adultery is sinful.

---

[27] Proverbs 6:27

Moreover, Jesus in His teachings on the subject stated, "*Whosoever looks on a woman to lust after her, hath committed adultery with her already in his heart*" (Matthew 5:28). He emphasized that "*Whosoever shall put away his wife, except it be for fornication, and shall marry another, commits adultery: and whoso marries her which is put away doth commit adultery.*"[28]

The biblical views on adultery show the serious implications since Jesus did not stop at overt adultery, but referred to the secret desires of the heart. Jesus was teaching the intents of the human heart by showing where the seed of adultery originates and germinates before it becomes an outward act.[29]

Adultery Affects the Entire Body

The Bible further declares that every sin that a man commits is outside of the body, but when that sin is adultery, that person sins against his own body. Not only does this sin affects the body, but it also grieves the Holy Spirit because the body is His temple (*See* 1 Corinthians 6:18-20). Furthermore, infidelity can be likened to a contagious disease that has infected the structural framework of marital relationships leading to all types of symptoms.

Practice Self-Control

Since the very thought of adultery is firmly forbidden by God, every Christian couple should maintain a standard of self-control, rather than being deceived by their flesh. Adultery is considered an exceedingly evil and wicked sin, which greatly displeases God.

The Law of God in the Old Testament considered adultery one of those terrible crimes worthy of death.[30] The adulterer was stoned or burned. Besides, in the early church, an adulterer faced immediate

---

[28] Matthew, 19:9; also Luke 16:18; Mark 10:2-12.
[29] *See* Proverbs 4:23; Matthew 15:19-20.
[29] See Genesis 20:3, 7, 17; Proverbs 2:12-15, 16-19; John 8:3-5.

expulsion.[31] I am not advocating drastic measures against adulterers since each person will face God at some time either here or in eternity.

On reflection, is the adulterer the only one guilty when adultery occurs? Often, this behaviour is the result of the denial of problems in the marriage. One of such problems is where one partner withholds sexual privileges from the other.

The Bible is strictly against this behaviour because it leaves a vacant opening for the enemy to enter into the relationship. God hates adultery, and spoke out severely against this act of disobedience to His Word.

Insensitive Wives

Many Christian wives are guilty of unfaithfulness because of their insensitivity, and reluctance to be loving and tender to their husbands. They seem to have lost all desires for sexual passion, even though their husbands have been faithful towards them.

Some have even put their so-called ministries before their husbands. In some of those situations, there are men who have maintained their marital responsibilities and have stayed with their unfaithful wives. Yes, I did say *unfaithful*.

We need to be honest and recognize that although adultery is an awful sin; some women do drive their husbands to the open arms of another woman. Since some wives can be subtly cruel with their vindictive behaviours we must be careful what we say when we hear that a man has committed adultery.

Lest the reader thinks that I am condoning a wrong, I am not promoting the behaviour of adultery. However, before we cast judgment against any situation, it is better to hear both sides since there are two people in the relationship.

Then again, there are adulterers who have ceased from their wanton behaviours, but their *Christian* wives refuse to forgive them of the past.

---

[31] 1 Corinthians 5:1-2, 9-12.

I would invite those wives to look at Calvary, and see Jesus dying there for their sins. Then ask themselves "Can I forgive........for what he has done to me?" When face to face with God, He will not ask about anyone else, but only the person standing before Him. Consequently, we each have to give account for our own selves.

The Bed is Undefiled

The Bible teaches that the marriage bed is undefiled. This means that if the couple maintains their Christian obligations, they should not have cause to be suspicious of each other. Marriage is holy; and obedience to the principles will keep the bed undefiled. This means there will be no introduction of unnatural behaviours or social impurities that will taint the spiritual setting of the relationship.

Chapter 19

Sexual Purity in Marriage

Sexual purity, coupled with active regular togetherness, is vital for the quality and stability of the marriage. However, if the couple base the marital relationship only on sex, when the novelty has worn off, and the euphoria dissipates, so will the relationship. The partners will be looking for new exploits to test their sexual dexterity because they have lost the desire to be with each other. Is it any wonder that many marriages have failed?

To look at marital sexual purity, it is important to note that the physical act is not sinful. Rather, it is biblical. Sex becomes sinful when this takes place outside the boundaries of marriage, whether the couple is Christian or non-Christian.

Additionally, the act of sex within the confines of marriage is not unholy, nor should it ever be seen as such. The Bible says, *"Marriage is honourable in all, and the bed undefiled..."* (Hebrews 13:4a). Yet, there are couples who consider sex to be something detestable.

When there are problems they do not talk about them, and if they have to face it, it is with dread. When an individual feels compelled to do something deemed dreadful, there will be struggles because that person cannot respond in the way that is expected.

However, it would not be fair to leave this spot without mentioning that there are reasons why some women dread the sexual act in marriage. It could be that they experienced sexual abuse in childhood, either in the form of molestation or rape. Usually this might have been with a close family member or friend.

Anyone who has been in either situation should seek help before entering into a marital relationship because reluctance and dread of sex can cause repercussions in the marriage leading to infidelity. Since the Bible affirms sexuality in marriage as sacred and the bed holy, blessed, and undefiled, there should be no dread in participating in this activity meant for marriage.

Sex is a natural feature of married life, but it must not be a tool to control one partner. This behaviour leads to sexual misconduct, and may even make a husband seek for someone who will treat him with the respect he needs.

However, such action is not right, and it is better to seek for intervention in the form of marital counseling to prevent the act of infidelity. Moreover, in order to maintain sexuality and prevent infidelity the Bible states that each person should have his/her own partner, and that each should render due benevolence to the other (*Scriptures mentioned earlier*).

Furthermore, fidelity in marriage will prevent the growing increase of sexually transmitted diseases that are so prevalent in this age.

With the presence of Acquired Immune Deficiency Syndrome [AIDS] and other diseases, let the sexually adventurous beware.

Still, taking care is not smart when one is breaking God's Laws.

Chapter 20

It is a Social Germ

The apparent universal acceptance of infidelity has led to the permissiveness and moral decay of society leading to the breakdown of marriages. Infidelity is an insidious and destructive behaviour that has destroyed the structure of marriage and family life. Is there any controversy then of its relationship to interpersonal conflict? It is a social disease affecting everyone in its path, particularly the family.

Similarity of Infidelity to the Common Cold

Indisputably, infidelity is as contagious to the family system, as the common cold is to the human body. Similar to the common cold, there seems to be no known cure for adultery, other than what God has stated in His Word that each man should have one wife and cleave to her alone. Obviously, a sincere monogamous relationship is the main answer for prevention of the breakdown of family life.

Again, analogous to the common cold that spreads from droplets, the environment that breeds adultery such as the media and pornographic literature causes it to affect marriages faster than the speed of sound and reaches to the entire expanse of the world. It has climbed to the highest peaks of leadership and economic status; and dropped to the lowest levels in society. It has crossed all the continents of the world.

Unmistakably, the sin of adultery has become one of the most powerful social germs that could have ever infected the institution of marriage. This is the most invasive, voracious, social epidemic to infiltrate the family system. It has no respect for culture, class, religious, or social barriers. The result of this leads to a breakdown in traditional family life.

The very act of infidelity destroys the moral values of trust, respect, loyalty, and integrity, good communication, and the spiritual values of the marriage covenant. It causes fear, anger, and frustration. This behaviour has become so prevalent, that not only men are guilty of this crime against marriage, but women too are high on the list of offenders.

Studies have shown that in a marital relationship both men and women are guilty of infidelity against each other. The report is that 25 to 75 percent of all males and 15 to 60 percent of women have admitted to having had affairs (Gerhardt, 1999; Buchanan, 1990).

This behaviour is not only prevalent in mainline society, but it has become a deadly evil in the church community. The prevalence of adultery among leaders and church members has become frequent occurrences and has made headline news. Some of those persons have been notable personalities who have disgraced their ministry, and reproached the name of Christ who called them.

Infidelity is a behaviour that has reduced the value once placed upon marriage, so that this institution has become a *revolving door*. Evidently, the freedom of sexual immorality has caused marriage to lose the meaning of fidelity. This was the key factor that kept it intact, preventing intruders from entering that sacred door.

Infidelity Hurts

Surprisingly, but people have become indifferent towards this behaviour, and only shrug their shoulders when they hear of someone who has committed this evil. Sometimes they display attitudes such as, "So what, he is not the only one who has committed adultery."

Attitudes such as those only make the pain of adultery more unbearable as it perpetuates the behaviour. In addition, there are emotional unimaginable hurts to both the victim, and the adulterer.

Admittedly, not everyone copes the same way with the emotional distress that is associated with infidelity. There are women who shake off the hurt, and just move on with their lives after the initial shock waves have subsided. Good for them!

- *I honestly wanted to get my revenge for what he had done to me and to our children.*
- *I recall going to the doctor regularly for symptoms that I did not notice before. It was horrible.*
- *I was devastated, and felt dirty because I did not know until it was too late.*
- *I felt sick in my mind. The discovery was nauseating.*
- *I was glad to be rid of him.*
- *I could not get out of the courtroom fast enough.*
- *Now I will be taking care of myself.*
- *I could not stand it any longer, and I knew that I did the right thing.*

Despite how a woman deals with the discovery, adultery is a tragic assault on the unsuspecting spouse and an indication of disrespect, selfishness, and betrayal. For this reason, some women will retaliate in like manner to get even with their husbands. Others turn their backs on the adulterer and consider him an enemy. Not surprisingly, there are those who remain in the home, if only to be a "thorn in his flesh."

Infidelity is Reckless

I ponder about the weaknesses in the structure of marriage today, and question what types of circumstances are causing this sudden thrust of immorality and irreverence to this institution.

What has infiltrated this once solid spiritual establishment that was the bedrock of a wholesome and strong family? The main answer that comes to my mind is infidelity because of the disrespect offenders place on family values.

I then ask the following questions. Why has infidelity become such a reckless behaviour to contaminate the sacredness of marriage? What are the causes for this gross insensitive behaviour? Do the perpetrators of infidelity think about their actions? Do they think about the people who will be hurt? What really goes through the mind of an adulterer?

Presumably, adulterers are of the opinion that what they do is their own concern, and their behaviour does not affect anyone else but themselves. This is indeed an erroneous belief because the effect of the sin of adultery touches everyone who is connected to the adulterer.

Nevertheless, some adulterers confess that they feel a sense of guilt at the initial stage of their behaviour; but after a while, the feeling wears off when the behaviour becomes habitual, and the deception has cemented.

Do adulterers understand that when they go to someone other than their wives that they put them at risk for getting diseases? There are serious consequences for adultery. Moreover, the discovery of adultery can shatter the entire stability of the home because it threatens the peace of mind of the wife and children. It also leaves deep, invisible, emotional, and psychological wounds that require professional and spiritual help.

Adultery and Domestic Violence

In addition, I have strong conviction, that the act of adultery is a form of domestic violence. The reason is that the violated person suffers emotional abuse that leaves deep invisible wounds. Someone may raise the question as to why I consider adultery to be domestic violence.

For example, the woman who remains with her unfaithful husband may have to put up with her husband's foul language, frequent absences, verbal threats, various forms of abuses, along with his insulting behaviour if she dares to challenge him about his adulteries. He may even reduce his financial support in the home to keep his mistress happy.

This means that the wife suffers, and so do the children. This is especially so in a situation where the wife does not go out to work. Furthermore, a mistress might be extremely demanding, and often the man feels obligated to please her before his wife.

Labels and Excuses

Another important point is the variety of pseudonyms and excuses given to the behaviour of infidelity, maybe to minimize its effect on the injured parties, such as the other spouse and children. It seems easier to say, *"Oh it was just a fling." "There was nothing to it." "Boys will be boys." "It's the mid-life crisis." "She is going through menopause…" "I only cheated once,"* and the labels and excuses go on.

Although those who engage in this activity may dream up palatable names for this dangerous social germ, there are people closely connected to the adulterer who suffer spiritually, emotionally, financially, and psychologically. Those persons include children, friends, family members, and wives who have chosen to remain with their unfaithful husbands.

Chapter 21

Some Reasons for Infidelity

Researchers are of the opinion that there is a combination of reasons for infidelity. However, those reasons are wide and varied. In some cases, there are cultural situations, coupled with the masculine ego. The issues range from personal low self-esteem, menopause, freedom of expression, to mid-life crises.

Accepting those reasons for making adulterers feel comfortable, seems deceptive and insubstantial. They describe persons who are self-centred and uncaring, especially in the case of the disabled and chronically ill. Besides, the deception places a tremendous psychological burden on the betrayed spouse (*See* Glass, 1998).

Since the primary principle for marriage is permanence with the indelible words "for better or worse, in sickness and in health, 'til death us do part," no one should use sickness or impairment as an excuse to commit adultery against a helpless spouse. *Some reasons include but not limited to the following*:

Inconsistencies in the Relationship

If a wife refuses her husband his conjugal rights, this conduct could make him stray from the marriage bed. For some wives, after the birth of a baby, there is reluctance to return to sexual activities with their husbands. Others have forgotten about sex, and have not returned at all even after many years of marriage. True! A few husbands might be patient, but there are those who do not take this type of treatment gracefully, and they may even consider this desertion in some extreme cases.

One reason why infidelity may infiltrate a marriage could also be that the woman suffers pain during intercourse, whether imagined or real, and this can lead to the act of infidelity. Unless that woman seeks professional treatment, her constant denial or aversion will make the husband become impatient, and he might feel neglected and begin to look outside for fulfillment.

Infidelity can also be a result of past abuses the woman experienced as a child or from a previous relationship that have left severe emotional scars she finds hard to cope with. Including are women who have suffered incest and rape, and the memory of those situations can become a barrier to their response. For those reasons, the woman is unable to respond to sex or receive her husband in a loving way.

Since sex is the ultimate in a marital bond, not being able to fulfill that aspect of the relationship can leave a man very hurt and angry. The constant rejection from his wife may even pose a threat to his manhood. There are indeed many reasons why infidelity will invade the marriage.

A Lesson from Nature

Nevertheless, when there are problems in the relationship causing the cold winds of marital storms to blow, the couple can learn a lesson from nature instead of taking the path to the divorce court. We have all seen the nakedness of the trees during autumn, and we have all felt the icy cold winds of winter with the frost biting at our extremities.

Yet, no one grieves over the trees that have lost their covering to the changes of nature. We do not despair because we know that in a few months time spring will come again. Everything needs time, and so does a marriage, especially a sick one.

Another analogy is from the animal kingdom. A pet lover finds it very difficult to put a well-loved, but sick animal to sleep. Yet that same individual will *gladly* kill or put a sick marriage to death. It would be just as rewarding to make every effort to heal a sick marriage and try to grasp the last dying shreds, rather than destroy what was once a good relationship.

Unresponsiveness

On a different note, while it is wrong to commit adultery, many spouses contribute to the other straying from the marriage. There are wives who are extremely cold and insensitive towards their husbands' sexual advances. They are unromantic, and lack the feminine lustre and attraction their husbands need to pursue them. They are plain, uninviting, uninteresting, and obviously unattractive to their husbands. Some husbands will complain that their wives show no interest in them or appreciation for even the gifts they bring home.

For instance, when a husband buys a bunch of flowers, a nice perfume, or a box of chocolates and the wife pays no attention, he feels very badly about her coldness. Some wives only say, "Thanks," and move on without a hug or recognition towards their husbands' effort in making them happy.

I am not even thinking of a husband who has already committed adultery in an effort of winning his wife's favours. I am referring to those men who want to keep their marriages intact and their wives happy.

Other wives refuse to go out, such as an evening out, dinner after church, or take a vacation with their husbands. Clearly, in many situations, the wives should take the blame for their husbands' adulteries.

Next, some wives will validate another man instead of their own husbands. I have met wives who would not speak a kind word about their husbands.

Obviously, if they do not speak kindly about them in public, how do they treat those men at home? How can they say that those men are bad? Let us be honest, it takes two people to break a relationship.

Chapter 22

Myths about Infidelity[32]

Typical of most situations that are wrong, there are various myths surrounding the attractions of infidelity. One of those myths states that adultery is *about sex*. This myth can be refuted because sometimes most of those extramarital relationships were only fatal attractions whereby a woman played her game and trapped a married man into falling for her.

Moreover, there are women who will testify that they prefer married men. Obviously, they do not have any reservations about trapping the unsuspecting prey. Usually, a neighbour or trusted "friend" is the culprit.

Did I say *friend*? That man is taken unawares as the fly to the spider's web, and only realizes when it is too late. Those men who have been deceived are to be found in the "who is who" of society both in the secular and Christian circles.

Secondly, adultery is about character. The man who loves his wife will not violate that trust. When adultery takes place, the perpetrator is making a statement that he no longer values the love and relationship he once had with his wife. He is saying that the sacredness of marriage means nothing to him.

In terms of character, this can be viewed from two perspectives. For instance, on the one hand there are men who believe that it is manly to have another woman with their wives. The intruder on the other hand,

---

[32] See Eaker-Weil, B.E. & R. Winter. *Adultery, The Forgivable Sin – Healing the Inherited Patterns of Betrayal in Your Family.* (A Birch Lane Press Book Published by Carol Publishing Group, 1993).

especially if she is younger may consider herself prettier than the wife. The intruder does not think of the hurt and pain she is causing and may vie with the wife for the husband with no shame or remorse. Character does play a vital role in the adulterous relationship.

Thirdly, that sex is therapeutic. The writers consider this third myth to be a misguided concept because "you cannot fix what's wrong with a relationship by adding another complication." It is a fact that adultery has some *ugly* turn-styles and outcomes, which cannot be considered character.

Incidentally, I have heard from young people that sex is indeed therapeutic because it relieves depression and stress. If that is so, it should be with one's spouse and not with someone outside of the marital relationship.

The *fourth myth* is that infidelity is harmless. By the time readers have read this book, they will understand that infidelity is not harmless. Usually, the act of adultery hurts innocent people when it infiltrates the relationship.

Children suffer the pain of separation from one parent and trying to compete with step-siblings and the new spouse. Wives have complained of being embarrassed about their husbands cheating habits. In some cases murders have been committed, and men have been incarcerated all because of what they thought was a *harmless* act. Over the years, I heard stories where lives have been lost, and incarcerations resulted because a mistress refused to let the affair end. Infidelity is destructive and costly.

This behaviour weaves an exceedingly deceptive web that tangles up everyone in its immediate path. It causes pain, shame, and remorse. It is not harmless. Of all the myths, this is extremely preposterous. Infidelity hurts innocent people because of the emotional and psychological consequences.

If you disagree with this, then ask those who have suffered the results of this behaviour. Each outcome may not be the same, but they are consequences nevertheless.

The *fifth* and final myth states that infidelity has to end in divorce. The writers noted, "If the real motivations for adultery are recognized, and the skills to deal with the underlying problems are learned, couples could overcome the trauma."

The main point is that the couple must learn to face the facts about the relationship, in order to discourage the need for revenge. They further add:

> Until we forgive the transgressor, we cannot get rid of our own anger, bitterness, and depression; we cannot feel hope and optimism...only when we reconcile can we start all over again (*See* Eaker-Weil, & Winter, 1993).

Therefore, adultery does not have to end in divorce if the partners can deal with the differences that led to the problems. There are marriages that have overcome and outlived the intrusion of adultery because the injured was willing to forgive, and the husband was truthful in turning his back on the mistress.

In some cases, faith, prayer, family members, children, close friends, and outside intervention were the key factors in bringing the marriage back together. There were also extreme cases where the husband became ill and he returned home to his *loving* and *patient* wife to nurse him back to health. Women like those are to be admired because they are truly examples of patience and longsuffering.

There are also cases where, although some husbands would want to return to their wives and children, yet some mistresses do not want to let go.

Those women cling to the men and do everything in their power to prolong the relationship. In such a situation, it takes a man who has truly repented to end the relationship despite the attractions.

I do not believe that all men set out to hurt their wives because many were innocent. What happened is that they were weak and fell for the women in their time of weakness. I am not making excuses for adulterers, but we must face the realities of life. Others have fallen headlong without care for the injuries to their wives or children.

Marriage is a partnership between a man and a woman. However, when there are children, whatever happens in the relationship will affect the entire family.

Adultery is definitely not harmless.

Chapter 23

The Charade

Sexual marital immorality has become an acceptable behaviour in society, so that the practice of monogamy no longer appears to be the norm, but the exception.[33] The assumption is that some men and women will have an extramarital affair sometime during the marital relationship. This point hardly needs empirical evidence because reports have shown that marital sexual immorality is rampant in all areas of society.

Although the desire of all marriage partners is for fulfillment, permanence, and monogamy, people do change, either for good reasons or for destructive ones. Some are adventurous with a careless attitude, while others are *just* curious and irresponsible.

Seemingly, they say to themselves, "Today, let us throw caution to the wind – let down your hair, be carefree, frolic, make love, and have our fill of sex, and bear the consequences tomorrow." Strange, but the biblical verse is so true. It says, *"...for whatsoever a man sows, that shall he also reap."*[34]

Consequently, if the individual sows to the wind that person will reap the whirlwind.[35] There are many evidences that the nation is now reaping the whirlwind from the reckless behaviours from the result of immorality. Children are struggling in an attempt to understand the disruption to their lives with questions that no one is able to answer.

---

[33] Vaughan, P. The *Monogamy Myth: A Personal Handbook for Recovering From Affairs.* (New Revised Edition, Copyright © Vaughan & Vaughan), 1999

[34] Galatians 6:7

[35] Hosea 8:7

Eventually, they take out their frustrations with the use of substances that are harmful to them or they will find some means of satisfaction to ease their pain.

For the most part, the social order has accepted the destructive behaviour of infidelity without much disapproval. This social immorality has taken up residence in all areas of society. For this reason, many women have kept silent about living with an adulterous husband. *Why make a fuss? Who cares anyway?*

In addition to the weakness of monogamy in society, the church itself is at fault since ministers have been found to be involved in improper sexual relationships.

Some have even been involved in homosexuality while in the pulpit, and still living with their wives. These are the cold facts that were once unheard of, but have now become factors in the breakdown of marriage.

Amazingly, despite the rise in infidelity, it has been noted that the belief in society is that monogamy is the norm.[36] This is indeed far from being the truth. One does not need a survey to understand the social corruption in the marital relationship because of the immoral behaviours of adulterers, both inside and outside of the church community.

Evidently, if the leaders in the church are guilty of this behaviour, obviously society will be even far worse. Many partners do not observe loyalty, honesty, and integrity in the relationship because there is no more surprise when one commits adultery.

Frankly, fidelity, even in the church community has become a principle that seems very difficult to uphold. Since there are women who actually set themselves up to deceive married men, and also men who have no qualms about confronting a married woman for an illicit

---

[36] Vaughan, P. The *Monogamy Myth: A Personal Handbook for Recovering From Affairs.* (New Revised Edition, Copyright © Vaughan & Vaughan), 1999

relationship which sometimes lead into sexual activity, why should anyone bother.

Nevertheless, when there is proof of infidelity, it should be an opportunity for the injured person to do some form of self-examination and ask, "Where did I come short? How did I contribute to this breakdown in *our* marriage?"

Pointing a finger at another person is not always the answer. Each one in the triangle is responsible for a portion of the blame in the breakdown of the relationship. Furthermore, when there are identifiable problems it is advisable to seek outside help to give the marriage another chance even after infidelity.

Apparently, monogamy in the marital relationship appears to be no longer the norm, but the exception. This is a sad truth to grasp because, in my mind, every couple wants the marriage to last. However when the crisis of infidelity occurs, some injured partners may decide to remain in the relationship with the hope that the behaviour will stop.

Regrettably, this is sometimes a disappointment if the adulterer continues with the behaviour. In some cases, the perpetrator may go on for years not caring how the other person feels or what the behaviour is doing to their marriage and family.

Although the sinful behaviour of infidelity appears to be fashionable in society, it has some very severe outcomes. Despite the fact that this lifestyle has become socially acceptable, it causes pain and many hurtful consequences.

The reason is that when the marital relationship fails, this is compounded by blame, shame, frustrations, and feelings of devastation. Many injured wives are often so ashamed, that they do not want anyone to hear that there are problems. Although wives suffer, there are those who remain with their unfaithful husbands.

Chapter 24

Why Men Cheat

Ironically, but many of the men who cheat will confess that they love their wives and do not want those wives to leave them. They will also admit that they have an insatiable appetite for sex, and that they cannot resist certain types of women.

Some men just love to take chances, and no matter what the consequences are, they will commit adultery. When confronted with their cheating some men will unashamedly tell their wives "I know that you will not leave me, no matter what I do."

If a man cheats, and believes he can get away with it because his wife does not seem to care, he will continue doing so by the so-called acceptance of his wife if she remains passive about the behaviour. It is in the interest of the woman to be proactive and to seek for help if she desires to remain in the marriage.

Clearly, men will cheat because either it is attractive or maybe they think, "My wife does not mind." Admittedly, the sin of adultery is not new. Nevertheless, it is socially established so that people just shrug their shoulders when they hear of this crime against marriage.

As was mentioned earlier, some men cheat because of their ego. However, there are those who do it because they believe that their wives will not leave them no matter what they do.

Corrine reported that her husband told her that he knows that she is a Christian woman and would not leave him, so he continues with his adulteries. Another husband told his wife that he could not be satisfied with one woman, and must have more than one to fulfill his sexual appetite.

Men commit adultery because of selfishness, and if they think, they will get away with the behaviour. Moreover, in the social setting, behaviours such as adultery are no longer a terrible crime against marriage. Instead, it is fashionable to have someone else other than one's partner.

A few decades ago, I was present at a wedding reception. I saw the groom dancing very happily with his "new" wife. However, there was another woman standing nearby. I asked, "Who is that woman?"

The response was, "The *other* woman." I was very young then, and to me this was unheard of. It would seem that to have a mistress with one's wife is a masculine entitlement. Additionally, it is usual to hear of men who have office "wives," and women with office "husbands." What will they think of next?

Some men are unfaithful because women make themselves available by enticing them. In some instances, there are women who will do the *femme fatale* act, if only to get into a man's arms. Women will behave in any way, if only to set a trap for the man maybe as retaliation because he deceived her and married another. Others do it to get promotion, for extra cash, and for various other reasons. Despite the reasons, hear what Solomon said about the seductress:

> For the lips of a strange woman drop as an honeycomb, and her mouth is smoother than oil: but her end is bitter as wormwood, sharp as a two-edged sword. Her feet go down to death; her steps take hold on hell...her ways are moveable, that thou canst not know them. Remove thy way far from her, and come not nigh the door of her house (Proverbs 5:3-8).

Therefore, we should not blame the men entirely, but the men should have courage to say "no."

Sometimes men allow their sexual addiction to overcome them, which is similar to that of any forbidden substance. For this reason, they will even leave their wives at home, go out, and pay for this physical social commodity.

113

Other reasons for committing adultery include unfulfilled desires, personal weaknesses, attention from other women, or even just for the fun of an interlude or adventure with sin.

Infidelity can be the result of many situations. However, there are no reasons for this behaviour to become an institutionalized norm in society. Infidelity is sinful, therefore wrong. There are severe consequences to everyone involved in this terrible crime against the once sacred institution of marriage.

Finally, although habitual adulterers have tarnished the sanctity of marriage, there are those married men and women who still hold the institution to be sacred and permanent. However, because of Jesus' death, burial, and resurrection, there is hope for the adulterer who truly repents and seeks pardon from God, and reconciliation with a spouse.

Men have been Programmed

Although infidelity is a terrible act, it would seem that some cultures expect men to be unfaithful to their wives, while the wives quietly accept the behaviour. One person told me, "It is usual for men in my culture to have other women even when they are married. It seems to be an unwritten law." This could be the way they were raised.

For instance, boys usually have the freedom to stay out late at nights with their friends. They are encouraged to sow their wild oats so that they *know* what to do when they are married. Is it any wonder that men behave the way they do when they are married? They are programmed how to behave with women from childhood, to have the upper hand with them.

In addition, in some homes young boys grew up seeing dad behaving immorally. Some of those fathers had children with different women and took no note of the types of behaviours they were displaying before their children, especially their sons. The perception of those children is that since the behaviour was all right with dad or mom, it must be the right thing to do.

Signs of an Adulterer

Many times wives will confess ignorance of their husbands' adulteries. They pretend and ignore signs of change in their behaviour. Even when the signs are sticking them in the eye, some wives will still defend their husbands, and deny that any cheating is going on.

Here are a few signs that women should look for in an adulterer's behaviour.

- He is the first to rush for the phone
- He muffles and whispers when taking a call
- He lies about who is calling. "Honey, who was on the phone?" "No one dear, it was a wrong number; telemarketing"
- The phone bill begins to increase
- He stays out late. [*Excuses*]
- The cell phone is off limits to you
- He suddenly takes special care with his dressing
- He has no time for you
- He is nervous when the phone rings
- He does not look you in the eye when you ask about a *certain* female
- He is rude and disrespectful to you
- He spends more time with the "boys"
- You suddenly find that he is not interested in sex
- He hurries when you have sex
- He is always tired when you pursue him
- He starts wearing different cologne
- He starts making comments about your dressing, looks, size…
- He is short-tempered, and picks a fight only to get out of the house
- He rushes out of the house pretending to avoid a fight

- He complains about the house, your cooking, the way you discipline the children
- He becomes picky about everything
- Church attendance becomes infrequent
- He no longer admires you. "Honey, do you like my new dress?" "I suppose it's all right," without looking you in the eye
- He leaves without telling you where he is going, or where he has been
- He suddenly brings you flowers, perfume, gifts. [*When he is about to be discovered*]
- You smell a different perfume in his car
- You find receipts from hotels, stores, florists, etc., which you know *nothing* about
- Suddenly, he has to work late three or four nights per week
- He takes un-scheduled trips
- He bought gifts, flowers that did not come home
- He gets annoyed over the simplest thing
- He cannot find his wedding ring. [*Because he left it in the hotel room*]
- He refuses to answer simple questions, and so on…

Chapter 25
Why Women Remain in Unfaithfulness
[Part 1]

The literature for the recent research conducted by this writer showed that existing studies have not explored deeply into the incidence of infidelity. Furthermore, many did not indicate why wives live with husbands who have been unfaithful.

Additionally, to be more specific, there seems to be an abundance of information on marriage, separation, and divorce. However, researchers have not yet delved intensely into the lives of women who experience infidelity, the interpersonal conflicts associated with this behaviour, and its aftermath.

This paucity of empirical evidence presents an implication to the study of women's affairs and reflects on both society and the church. It conveys a meaning that this area of women's study is not as important as other areas for social researchers to investigate.

Moreover, it would seem that even church leaders have fallen short of helping hurting women. Members will testify that many leaders are more interested in certain aspects of membership, but other areas do not seem as important.

For example, when a husband walks out, divorces his wife, and leaves his children, the woman [member] faces the estrangement by herself. How many of those leaders or members in any particular church take the time to counsel that woman, or walk with her in her lonely shoes? Does that woman get emotional support from the church?

Honestly speaking, for the most part, all that the women will hear are spiritualized snippets such as, "We will be praying for you." "This is a trial or test," or some other spiritual plaster to heal the wound left by the break.

Do not get me wrong. I am not here to hammer at church leaders or their members. My intention is to *provoke* leaders and members of churches to be more *sensitive* to those persons who are going through losses and abandonment. Many women who are living with their unfaithful husbands have been so humiliated and ashamed, so that even if they wanted to talk with someone, fear is the leading factor that prevents them from doing so.

One of the reasons why some members are fearful is because church members have a way of *distributing* private personal information to their friends, especially those who are in cliques. Oh, some of them can be very busy with their mouths. Is it any wonder that many members keep quiet about their personal problems?

Obviously then, the reports of the women in this study give clear indication that their voices ought to be heard. They have been silent for a long time, and now here is an opportunity for others who are still facing the shame and humiliation of living with unfaithful husbands to know that they are not alone.

The fact that their husbands are willing to trade their sacred vows for a moment of passion or sexual pleasure shows a lack of good judgment and consideration for their actions, and gross disrespect for their wives and children. If thought was given to the consequences for infidelity with the resulting disappointments, many people might not have been caught up in this behaviour.

It is without question that women will experience immediate relief by delaying their response to interpersonal conflict, upon the discovery of infidelity. However, this will be short-lived because when people deny or avoid conflicts, then there is the likelihood that resentment and hostility will take over. Those are factors akin to interpersonal conflicts. Nevertheless, it is often better to delay anger, rather than let the emotion get out of hand.

First impressions may present the woman as being foolish for her decision to stay in the relationship. However, after listening to the women, they related many significant reasons for making the choice for remaining instead of divorcing their husbands. The decisions may seem ridiculous and insignificant to some readers, but until the person enters the world of another, it is better to be less critical and more empathetic and understanding.

Regardless of how some adulterers feel about their wives, those women will affirm that adultery produces a type of pain that has no fair label that can describe such an assault to their emotions. Women agreed that living with an unfaithful husband is like having allergies. Similar to allergies, this pain is *seasonal*.

The women reported that some days they are able to overcome the shame and get on with their lives, whilst at other times it is just unbearable. Each day is uncertain, and life seems to be a risk with both their emotional stability and their state of mind. For this reason, many women have remained silent about the experience of infidelity because it seems that the behaviour is no longer a sin or violation of sacred marital trust.

The reasons include the following:
Investment
During a couple of the interviews, some of the participants were very upset. According to one woman, she had invested many years working to provide for the home and family. She commented on the time and money she spent buying things to maintain the home.

Despite the contributions, her husband openly had an affair with another woman, without shame or remorse for his behaviour or respect towards her or their children. As I sat and listened I boiled on the inside but had to control my emotions.

In fact, all the women pointed to investment as one of the reasons for staying. Can anyone blame them? It seems odd, but how can a man feel comfortable knowing that his wife has invested years, money, love, and so

on in the home; yet he disregards her contributions and go out to have affairs. Some of those men are very open with their behaviours because they do not care what they do, or whom they hurt. Some will even let the women call them at home.

Undoubtedly, you are telling yourself that there is clear evidence of infidelity in situations where there is proof. It is true that the woman has every reason to divorce the man. However, let us try to see this situation from the perspectives of any woman faced with this dilemma. It seems hard to give up years of financial investments to an adulterous man and his newly found love. Still, being strong in such a situation is not the answer.

Even so, how does one counsel a woman who finds herself in this situation? What words of encouragement can any person offer her? Should she count her losses and give up, or wait it out? This is a matter best left with the woman and God. I cannot deny that my emotions were stimulated while I listened to the participants, and no doubt, you too, can attest to the same rush of adrenalin as you read the reports.

While we may not know what to say, a keen listening ear, will help if the woman is able to trust someone with whom to relate her story. A word of warning, whether you are a family member or close friend; *never ever*, make a negative remark against the woman's husband. Avoid doing so, no matter how tempted you may feel. You may live to regret it!

Added to the infidelity, is to face the emotional pain of giving up one's earnings to someone who obviously no longer cares. What makes it worse is that those men are free to do whatever they desire because the woman might not want to jeopardize the relationship of her young children if she has any, with the father, or her position in her church.

Young children do not see any gray colours when there are problems in the home. Just seeing daddy, no matter how seldom he appears, is sufficient to gladden their hearts. Older children will be more aggressive, and will take a stand for or against one of the parents.

One woman did not invest money, but she stayed home and took care of a child while her husband educated himself. At the end, he betrayed her, and they ended up being divorced.

It is very sad to hear of women who have worked hard holding down two jobs, while a husband studies and improves himself. Yet, at the end of it all, he walks out and leaves her *penniless, barefoot, and poor*! Can you imagine that added to the investment, and devotion he files for a divorce because of his infidelities? This is enough to make any woman angry.

If your husband wants to better himself, so should you. Stop being naive and making martyrs of yourselves. When God said the man is the leader and the woman the helper, He did not mean domination! When He said the wife should submit to her husband, I do not believe that He meant for her to be a floor-mat.

Still, women ought to take heed, because there are extenuating circumstances when a divorce will be justifiable. God hates divorce, not the divorcee. We have to keep in mind that God who ordained marriages, knew that *not all marriages would* last. Let us face it; God knows everything!

Unfortunately, some churches are adamantly against divorce, no matter who is at fault or how evident the adultery. In any case, how does one console or advise those women who maintain the position of remaining in a marriage when infidelity has produced a child? Where is the blame? How should those women respond to this child, who will obviously visit the home if the father remains?

In the research, I encountered several women who reported that their husband's extra-marital affair produced a child. Some acts of infidelity have *long* shadows that will never disappear. They remain like scars for

121

many years to torment as they intensify the blow inflicted on the injured person. Unless God Himself applies His grace to soothe and console a woman in such a situation, she may become bitter and hostile against the child.

The only way an injured woman can help herself is to forgive the man and ask God's help to love him, despite his adulteries and the outcome. I am not saying to be *"romantically involved"* with him, but rather, to love him with the love of the Lord. This does not mean that they cannot make up and resume their relationship if the man truly repents and has made a full circle for change.

Furthermore, there are things we *cannot* change; and therefore we *have* to live with them. For this reason, forgiveness and love are the only balance that will keep the woman from hating her husband and the child produced from his behaviour. Obviously, even if there is a child from the affair, no woman would want to give up her home, and the years of investments, she has put into the relationship.

Continues on the next chapter.

Chapter 26
Why Women Remain in Unfaithfulness
[Part 2]

Paternal Presence

Another woman stated that she met her father for the first time in her later years. Although he provided for her all through those years, she had never seen him face-to-face. For this woman, the lack of a father figure in her life was one of the most disappointing memories of her childhood.

> When I met my husband, who was older, I was willing to do anything to keep our marriage going, especially after we had our children. Regrettably, he changed after five stormy years and started having affairs. He even took away my rings and threatened to bring the woman home for me to see that he was having an affair. I remained in the marriage because my intention was to give my children the presence of a father figure in the home.

The sacrifices a mother will make for her children at the expense of her own happiness are immeasurable. This is especially so when that woman is determined to forfeit personal feelings in exchange for her children's comfort and completeness. Some might ask if this was a good reason to remain in that situation. Again, how can anyone sit in judgment against the decisions a mother will make to keep her children happy?

Environmental Influence

I do believe that the silence by some women who live in adulterous relationships is the result of shame and the response the society gives to adultery. The reason is that, it is from the environment that we learn most of our social norms. That environment begins from the home, to the community, church, and school.

If a child knows that dad has had extramarital relationships, and there are children born from the relationship, while mom says nothing and remains with him, it gives an indication that it is all right.

Today, the internet and television programs are the major teachers of immorality and infidelity. It is from those environmental social settings that behaviours and norms are learned. Unless a child learns to discriminate when choosing behavioural patterns, that child will assimilate whatever seems natural, feels good, and comes easily.

Additionally, it would be fair to say that society trains us to underestimate emotional conflicts. Those situations are real and the injured can become violent because of the emotional pain. Whatever the reasons might be, infidelity is still sinful and immoral.

Therefore, the behaviour must not be rationalized with arguments to make the guilty feel comfortable. Indeed, infidelity must be viewed for its sinfulness; and therefore, it must be dealt with instead of being covered up or ignored.

Financial Security

The decision a woman makes to remain in an unfaithful marriage for financial reasons may seem plausible and selfish. Nevertheless, if there are young children who will go to college or other losses that might incur if the marriage is broken, then why not! If the woman can waive her husband's inconsistencies as she enjoys all the facilities he has to offer while coping with his infidelities, I repeat, "Why not!"

For instance, take the highly paid professional man and the wife who stays at home and does not go out to work. There are also wives, who are married to politicians or members of the clergy, who believe it is to their advantage to remain rather than choose the path of divorce.

Furthermore, there are not many situations where women earn more than men do. Actually, there are times when both women and men are doing the same jobs, but the men are paid more.

However, with the new technologies and the advancement in education, a few women sometimes do exceed some men. Although women have made great strides in changing their once inferior position, I would hypothesize that the margin is wide and the women still have a *lot* of catching up to do.

In addition, there are wives who remain only to be a thorn in the man's flesh because if there were a divorce, he would lose out. Those situations do happen and are indeed true. Reader, do not scoff at this. Still, *there are no winners with infidelity.* It comes with its own pains, crosses, and tragic circumstances!

> My husband pays all the bills and he provides for us, even though we hardly see him. Despite his infidelities, he does not cause us to suffer financially and he sees to it that the house is kept in good repairs. I receive whatever I want from him...

It would not be too extreme to think that many women would agree that to remain in an unfaithful situation for financial reasons is not a disgrace. It is possible that the woman has thought it all out in her mind, and she is willing to make this sacrifice for her own financial security.

Additionally, keeping the union intact, if only nominally, gives some women prestige and keep them in the position to which they have become accustomed.

Most of the women who remain in an adulterous marriage have purposed in their hearts that they will not marry again. Some women are middle-aged or grandmothers who feel satisfied with the warmth and love of their grandchildren. *Those women are not interested anymore in making new romantic encounters.*

Clearly, if the women can remain in the situation with a healthy spiritual, emotional, and psychological framework while spending their husband's money lavishly on themselves – *more power to them. I say, go for it girls!*

Continues in the next chapter.

Chapter 27
Why Women Remain in Unfaithfulness
[Part 3]

Fear of being Alone

Fear can be a crippling condition that will ensnare women into accepting situations that they otherwise could change. The fearful person becomes a prisoner to what she thinks might happen, and not what has happened. For example, the woman who is fearful of being alone, puts up with her husband's infrequent visits and responds to his advances when he comes home.

Nevertheless, although some women will go through the act of lovemaking after adultery, they are un-responsive, un-emotional, and show no romantic interest in the session. They just go through the motion of fulfilling their duty like an immovable rock in a river that lets the water splashes over it, *unperturbed*. They let the moment pass like a storm in the night, which they have no power to control. It is like, *services rendered!*

Another reason for fear could be losing the home. Many times divorce results in a home being sold to pacify the divorcees. Not many husbands will do the chivalrous thing to give up the home for the benefit of the wife and/or children.

In some situations, men have become hard and insensitive against women, and they have blamed their behaviour on the new feminist movement. Do they have a case? Who knows? Women have themselves complained that some have exchanged the glory of their femininity to obtain equality with men.

Regrettably, there are women who have even taken extreme measures to be equal with men, in order to reach their goals. As in everything else, there are good points and bad points. You be the judge.

Contrastingly, some women do believe that men should be leaders in the home, and they will do anything to maintain that support. Therefore, when the incidence of infidelity occurs, the woman can become fearful of losing that leadership role. Besides, some women are very dependent on their husbands, and the fear of losing them would mean losing half of themselves.

I have seen women fall apart after the death of a husband because they did not know what to do about paying bills, hammering a nail, and doing simple things that some women take for granted. Their fear of losing the husband, cause them to remain in the relationship even in the face of infidelity. They accommodate the behaviour and remain quiet.

Fear can also be a result of the unknown future, criticism from friends and relations, loss of social status, losing the children, and having to start all over again in a new relationship. Those are serious factors, which would motivate a wife to turn her face the other way and ignore her husband's unfaithfulness towards her.

Infidelity destroys marriages because of its destructive nature on the stability and value to the relationship. Therefore, re-building a marriage after an affair will present one of the most difficult tasks a couple will face.

Values

It is hard to give up values and personal beliefs, even if doing so would bring relief from hurt and pain. The wife, who places values before breaking a marriage, may find it very difficult to break the marriage vows. Some of those values reported by the women include religious, love, and personal.

- Although my husband is an adulterer, and still actively involved with other women, I will not divorce him, because I believe that marriage is a sacred covenant for life.
- When I took my vows I meant every word I said, and in any case, I took them before God. I cannot divorce him…
- I do not believe in divorce. It is wrong.
- I have been tempted several times to divorce him, but I just cannot make up my mind.
- The Bible says marriage is "'til death us do part" and whatever my husband does, I am going to uphold those principles.
- I cannot divorce my husband because we have children and they need their father.
- The church does not believe in divorce.

Personal and religious values go very deeply, and most women are not willing to allow infidelity to mar those principles.

Love

Another factor that can make a wife remain with her unfaithful husband is the love that still resides in her heart, despite his behaviour. Sincere love will remain even when there are apparent reasons for the wife to turn against her husband (*Compare* I Corinthians 13). Furthermore, in the face of hurt and anger, love can still survive as she reminisces on history, shared events, and loving scenes. Moreover, deep within her mind the wife still believes that by being patient, there is hope for the survival of the marriage.

This is understandable, especially in the case of Christian women and those who do not want to take the route of divorce as a means of escape. It would seem that those women have a strong relationship with God, and they are willing to maintain their faith in Him to heal the damaged marriage.

Spite

I have seen one situation where a woman remained with her husband after his infidelities, but still harboured animosities against him. Her hatred has remained after many years of living with him in the same house.

The aim was to gain revenge and to make his life miserable which she did successfully. His ministry did not grow but travelled down a spiral staircase. If the basis of the decision to remain is for selfish motives to spite a husband, then this act of malevolence will only hurt the injured wife, even if she got even with her husband. This would be a vindictive and senseless behaviour. In fact, it increases the hurt and the pain making them, even worse.

Women in such situations live in constant torment and misery. It is not hard for the onlooker to see the frustration and confusion on their faces. The moment someone approaches them, the marks of hatred and the wrinkles of unforgiveness intertwined on their faces, spiraling down from forehead to mouth to chin. There is evidence of a miserable spirit and irritation.

Those women hasten their ages, and spoil their own beauty as their facial appearance loses attractiveness and softness. There is no poise in their behaviour because they have difficulty responding in a pleasant manner.

Despite the realistic or non-realistic reasons for remaining with an unfaithful husband, it would be wise for each woman who faces this decision, to consider the *real* reason for doing so.

Part IV
Consequences of Infidelity

But whoso commits adultery with a woman lacks understanding: he that doeth it destroys his own soul. A wound and dishonour shall he get: and his reproach shall not be wiped away (Proverbs 6:32-33).

The Section covers the following Themes
- Infidelity is Destructive
- Spiritual
- Psychological
- Emotional
- The Family Re-defined
- Divorce Hurts Children

Chapter 28

Infidelity is Destructive

Despite its seeming attractiveness, the pervasiveness of infidelity results in some devastating and destructive outcomes. According to writers, infidelity is compared to an emotional assault that inflicts profound wounds on the injured party.[37] The consensus among writers is that infidelity leads to spiritual, psychological, emotional, and physiological problems.[38]

Furthermore, infidelity creates a plaque on the marriage that only the Blood of Jesus Christ can erase. Additionally, it leaves scar tissues in the mind of the injured, which requires sincere love and forgiveness, for some measure of recovery for the wounded.

The consequences of infidelity are great because its discovery reaches to the very soul of the injured person, resulting in both intra-psychic and interpersonal conflicts. The truth is that everyone feels those consequences because the adulterer is living under emotional strain with the knowledge that he is hurting his family, even though he may use every opportunity to conceal his behaviour from them.

Upon the discovery, the wife will question whether she is still attractive and asks herself, "Why?" as she struggles with the unshakable shame and remorse. Some of those unfaithful husbands are bold in telling their wives "You are too fat or too old," or "I am a man and can do what I want." Those painful words will emotionally wound a woman to the core of her heart.

---

[37] (Neal, 1999; McBurney, 1998; Eaker-Weil & Winter, 1993; Brown, 1991)

[38] (Vaughan, 1998; Eaker-Weil and Winter, 1993; McDowell 1993; Spring, 1993; Brown, 1991; Duck, 1991; Buchanan, 1990).

There are wives who can testify of receiving verbal abuses from their husbands, when they challenge them about their adulteries. For some of those women the "other" woman is a neighbour or friend. Such situations make the trauma even more painful. The wife agonizes with emotional torment seeing the woman who lives so closely, yet shows no remorse or concern for her feelings.

Reports from women:

- *I discovered that he was having an affair with someone whom I later found out was the next door neighbour...*
- *When I confronted him, he said it was none of my business.*
- *I was crushed, and felt like venting my feelings; but he seemed so stern and acted ugly. Therefore, I kept quiet and held my tongue.*
- *He took our child with him when he goes to see his girlfriend.*
- *He comes home only to change his clothes, but his friend lives next door. I was shocked when I heard.*
- *I found out that he has a woman in the same apartment building where we are living...*
- *My husband told my child "meet your new mother."*
- *I heard that the lover lives across the street from us.*
- *She was a friend of mine. I did not know that she was having an affair with my husband.*
- *I do not want to be close to him anymore.*
- *I would not know what to say or do.*
- *I am just not interested.*
- *He makes me sick.*
- *I am afraid of getting a disease.*

The excerpts are results of the *dark unexposed* side of infidelity and the harm it brings with it. Indisputably, infidelity does leave deep invisible scars that are indelible, and only the Blood of Jesus can remove them and heal the damaged emotions of those who hurt so deeply.

One husband told his wife after she confronted him, "It is none of your business what I do." Those words shattered her and made her depressed and stressful.

132

Women in those situations will only become more depressed, insecure, and anxious each day wondering what will happen next. Some wonder if there will be another child from the outside relationship, while others have experienced great humiliation and ridicule, sometimes from the other woman.

Ruth told of how a woman would call every day to torment her. After complaining to her husband, the calls stopped, but not the adultery. In some cases, the wife receives physical abuse from her husband if she complains about his behaviour and absences.

Another husband might even deny the fact that he is having an extramarital affair. Some husbands will try to confuse the woman by telling her that she is crazy to think such thoughts. This only leaves the woman more confused than she was before finding out about his behaviour.

Undoubtedly, infidelity causes interpersonal conflicts to occur, and this will affect the stability of the marital relationship. No matter how strong and indifferent the woman might be, she will react at some time in response to her emotions. Those conflicts can result in severe situations and many people get hurt.

Yet, the presence of conflict does not cause problems, but the wrong handling of an event will cause conflict to occur. The consequences of infidelity fall into four main categories that are spiritual, psychological, emotional, and health.

However, this is not conclusive since the consequences are many, with varying types of results that women living with their unfaithful husbands will experience. The ones listed here were emergent themes from the research carried out by this writer.

Chapter 29

Spiritual

The spiritual consequences resulting from infidelity will make the woman think negative thoughts concerning her relationship with the Lord. This can also cause her to neglect her duty in the church. In some severe situations, the woman's confusion can make her extremely bitter towards men.

There are women who are totally against re-marrying after being insulted by the infidelity of a husband. Still, if the woman is determined to keep her faith in God, she will recognize that infidelity is a tool of Satan to destroy marriages.

In the research carried out, the women pointed out that they considered their husbands' behaviour to be an attack of spiritual warfare. However, unless the woman has a close relationship with the Lord, she will succumb to the attacks of the enemy, and hatred will take the place of *forgiving love*.

I say here *forgiving love* because it is hard for some women to return to their husbands in a loving romantic way. Yet, this is not inconceivable. Other than hatred, the woman will also experience intra-psychic conflict as she struggles with the choice to please God, or to vindicate her own cause.

The woman might want to fight with her husband when he comes home late, forgetting that the "...*weapons of our warfare are not carnal, but mighty through God to the pulling down of strongholds*" (II Corinthians 10:3-4).

What many people do not understand is that, many so-called Christian women live separate lives from their husbands. They are hurting, but they pretend with a "business as usual" spiritual attitude.[39] The reason why many live this way is that they fail to forgive and to let go of the past.

Here is an example of forgiveness

Shelley had been married for only a few months, when she discovered that her husband had returned to his former lover whom he had before he met her. Apparently, she knew nothing about the previous relationship, and did not expect that her husband, a professed Christian could have been that deceiving. That marriage ended in divorce soon after the discovery. The Lord then spoke to Shelley to forgive the other woman. It was hard at first. One Sunday, the woman saw her and greeted her. Shelley said that she did not respond. She reported that when she got home, she was convicted and asked the Lord pardon. According to her, she promised that she would make up with the other person, and she did.

Impossible, no, with God, all things are possible. Anyway, there are women who have forgiven their husbands and have adopted children from their adulterous behaviours. *Forgiveness is possible after infidelity when problems are turned over to the Lord.* Furthermore, holding on to a grudge helps no one. Instead, it hurts only the unforgiving person.

The discovery of infidelity can also make the injured woman very angry, violent, and abusive; but those types of behaviours will separate her from God as she remains in bitterness. Anyway, the wife who holds onto an unforgiving spirit alienates herself from God. The devil blinds her eyes with resentment and malice that culminates into outbursts of anger and verbal abuse towards her husband.

The emotion of resentment can become a heavy load, and the woman finds it hard to pray, making her relationship with God weak as her prayer life sinks to almost zero. It is also possible that a woman in this situation can become very cynical and pessimistic towards religion and her faith in God.

Undoubtedly, infidelity *is* indeed a spiritual warfare attack on Christian marriages. It is therefore important for wives to understand,

---

[39] See *"When the Circle Breaks"* by this Author.

that although their husbands have committed a sinful act, the enemy is using those men for his purpose. The enemy has influence over their lives and he directs them to do what he wants. He dominates the lives of unfaithful husbands, and they move according to his impulse because they are not able to overcome his attacks. It is clear that those men are motivated by satanic stimuli.[40]

What the Christian wife needs to do is to counter attack by keeping in good relationship with the Lord through fasting, prayer, and seeking His direction in everything (*See* Proverbs 3:5-6).

Although the husband might not change; by acknowledging God with consistency, and having His peace that transcends all human understanding (*See* Philippians 4:7), the woman can have inner fortitude and tranquility as she sails through the rough seas of infidelity.

Unquestionably, living with an unfaithful husband will mean being tested to the ultimate because the wife is sharing her husband with another woman and in some cases, with a man.

The experience will also test the Christian virtues of the fruit of the Spirit (Galatians 5:22-23). These are spiritual warfare weapons to crush the demons of hatred, malice, resentment, and strife, which are connected to interpersonal conflict.

Essentially, the Christian wife should use the spiritual weapons (*See* Ephesians 6:12-18) in order to overcome satanic attacks, rather than become a victim of the enemy's assault. The Bible states that *"...in all these things we are more than conquerors through him that loved us"* (Romans 8:37).

Admittedly, the enemy will use the husband and overcome him, but he should not gain that authority over the Christian wife who is trusting in a God who cannot fail; the marriage might, but God will never fail.

Unfortunately, some Christian wives are not willing to see the attack of the enemy in their marriages and they in turn, attack their husbands.

---

[40] Ephesians 6 identifies the real enemy

In one situation, a wife told her husband when he was leaving the bedroom, "Go and don't come back." She stated that he never returned until the marriage ended in divorce. In fact, she ended up leaving the house. This Christian wife did not commit adultery, but her lack of wisdom cost her very dearly.

Indeed, the unwise conduct of Christian wives will only make their husbands more determined to continue with their adulterous behaviours. Furthermore, God will not hear their prayers to change the husband or heal the marriage.

In some severe situations, the woman may think that God is punishing her for past sins, especially if she thinks that no one cares about her. The spiritual consequences of adultery are spiritually damaging and costly to the Christian wife.

What is most important is for the injured wife to maintain a firm and consistent relationship with the Lord. He will always sustain her, but she must depend on Him and put her trust in Him. God does not fail, even when the marriage fails.

Chapter 30
Psychological
[Part 1]

Another consequence of infidelity is expressed in various forms of psychological problems. Some of those are the result of unresolved situations held over from childhood.[41] This situation shows up in maladaptive behaviours such as frequent outbursts of anger and silence towards the other partner.

There are also problems with depression, anxiety, stress, and psychosomatic disorders. These usually cause interpersonal conflicts in the marital relationship, especially at the time of the discovery of infidelity when the woman is confused and frustrated.

In some cases, unresolved childhood memories of abuse can prove to be destructive when taken into marriage. Those memories are often used as protective devices to prevent the individual from making firm commitments because of fear of being hurt again. The aggrieved wife will find it very difficult to separate this new injury from past situations, and might include them as her lot in life.

Infidelity can shatter whatever self-esteem the wife has built since those earlier injuries unless she has learned to accept herself and believe that God still loves her. The trauma of infidelity is deeply wounding, more so for those wives who have personal beliefs about marriage, its commitment, and permanence. For example, the wife who considers marriage to be a sacred covenant will find it very difficult to divorce her husband, despite his adulterous behaviours.

---

[41] (See Sarason and Sarason, 1996; Eaker-Weil and Winter, 1993; Brown, 1991).

Still, when infidelity secretly gains access into the marital relationship, the discovery of the deception creates tremendous psychological problems to the betrayed spouse. In this case, a wife may even think she is losing her mind because of the overwhelming intensity of concerns, sense of terror, anguish, feelings of despair, distress, and helplessness that she feels concerning her husband's infidelity.

Reports from women:

- *When I discovered his infidelity, I became tensed, cold, and unresponsive to his demands.*
- *There were times when the least thing would irritate me and made me cry. I could not bear for him to touch me.*
- *I spent many nights praying that God would heal the marriage. Some mornings when I wake up, I would be angry with God for keeping me alive. I did not want to live if He did not heal the marriage.*
- *There were nights when I could not sleep because I was crying all the time. I just could not compose myself to settle my mind.*
- *I would lay awake at times wondering why I had married this man, whilst the tears fall incessantly.*
- *I do not know of any pain that is as hurtful as being deceived by a husband. It seems unbearable. I often felt as if my heart would fall out of my chest because of the weight I carried around in my bosom. The shame and disappointment were heavy to bear.*
- *I begged him to let us work it out because I still wanted the marriage to last despite his unfaithfulness, but he was determined to destroy the relationship. What made matters worse, I found out that he was planning to divorce me...*
- *After a while, I was just going through the motions of living. I lived one day at a time as if I am in a dream.*
- *I withdrew from my friends and kept to myself most of the time. I did not want them to know anything about what I was going through. It seemed so personal that I did not seek for help. I lost all interest in my personal appearance and only did what was necessary...*

When a woman gets to the place where she no longer cares about herself or how she looks, it is a dangerous sign of despair. Infidelity brings dreadful consequences that the injured person finds very hard to face.

What is even more disturbing, is the woman who has separated herself from friends and family who could give her the emotional support that she needs at such a distressful time. However, this separation is not always self-inflicted.

- *When I asked my father for support, he virtually told me that it was my fault. I felt crushed and alone because I thought he would have been there for me.*
- *A friend told me, "You ought to have known better than to have married him."*
- *Members in my church criticized me. I was even told that I was too quick in getting married. Maybe I was hasty. In any case, I do not think people should be so hurtful when someone is facing problems. People just don't think sometimes.*
- *When my problems started, all I could remember were the harsh, critical words* a friend said to me.
- *I repressed everything, so that now I can't remember most of them.*

Continues in the next Chapter

Chapter 31
Psychological
[Part 2]

Cognitive Dissonance

Another psychological situation is cognitive dissonance. Festinger 1963 describes the condition as "the non-fitting relations among cognitions," also that "it is a motivating factor in its own right." This condition is really a feeling of discomfort when life suddenly brings on new events that disturb the peace of mind. Usually, those events do not make sense, because they disrupt a peaceful existence.

In the case of infidelity, the injured woman struggles with both negative and positive thoughts that create psychological tension. She is used to having her husband home at a certain time, someone who was a loving, attentive, kind, and warm man. Suddenly, without notice his behaviour changes and the wife cannot understand what took place to bring about such a drastic transformation of events.

She compares those cognitions or knowledge about herself, the marriage, and her husband with the presenting situations, but cannot find proper cause for his disloyalty. This lack of meaning from the thoughts leads to intra-psychic conflicts that obviously disturb her peace of mind.

In order for the woman to gain control of her thoughts and to find meaning for the presenting circumstances, she might appraise the event and make decisions to ease the internal conflicts.

Those thoughts, whether negative or positive will motivate her to take action to relieve the psychological tension she feels. Those tensions could be in the form of psychosomatic symptoms, headaches, insomnia, and other situations that cause distress because of the husband's betrayal.

Frequently, problems are the results of misunderstandings between partners and their appraisal of issues that develop in the relationship. It could be differences of opinions making one person stuck on personal beliefs and values. Those opinions could be a negative assessment of an appraisal about an event.

Moreover, it could be the result of disappointing information about a situation resulting in frustration, emotional, mental, and psychosomatic disorders.

Clearly, cognitive dissonance leads to intra-psychic conflict, which is one of the psychological problems that a wife who remains with her unfaithful husband might face. Each day she wrestles with her thoughts and the emotions, because of the internal inconsistencies in her mind. Eventually she will express the results of those thoughts in her attitudes and behaviours. As she struggles with the internal musings whether to leave her husband or remain, there is confusion because of those conflicting thoughts.[42]

Listen to the Reports.[43]

- *For a while, I thought about leaving him, but because of the church, I was not willing to do this. I struggled with this decision so that I could hardly sleep at nights. I knew that I should have left him, but just could not bring myself to do so.*
- *I thought about leaving him years ago, but I had nowhere else to go and I was not financially stable, so I endured the constant barrage of insults and harassment from his women friends...*
- *I threw him out of the house several times, but each time he came back. I could not help taking him back even though I knew that it was only a temporary make-up and I should not do it. I just could not make up my mind.*
- *I stayed with my husband because of my Christian beliefs. I hurt all the time and sometimes just feel that I would give in.*

---

[42] Compare Romans 7 with intra-psychic conflict

[43] *All the names in this book are fictitious, and the details are slightly changed.*

- *I just could not divorce him because I did not want to leave the church or displease God. I was so confused at times that I could not think properly.*
- *I wanted him out of my life, but I have contributed so much to this home that I am not willing to give it up to another woman.*
- *There is emptiness all the time. There is such a void that I do not know how to fill.*
- *It has been like a sword in my bosom. I believe it is my lot in life so I have to bear it.*
- *Sometimes I totally ignore him and I don't answer when he is speaking to me. I know it is wrong, but...*
- *I hate him and he knows it. I know this is wrong, but I cannot help it.*
- *Despite my feelings when he is home, he is company in the house.*
- *I did pray that God would kill him because he was abusing me physically along with his adulteries...*
- *I hate him...*

Positive dissonance

Additionally, the presence of cognitive dissonance can have either a positive or a negative outcome. The positive side of cognitive dissonance occurs when the injured wife thinks of positive ways that will change her perception of the circumstances that are causing the tension and turmoil in her mind.

For example, if the woman decides to accept the good points of her husband and trusts God to intervene in the situation, this belief might give her some relief and consolation to hope for a changed situation and a future stable relationship.

Furthermore, if the husband confesses to his behaviour, and promise to be faithful, the wife might feel a sense of security as she tries to re-build trust and give him another chance. Does this always help? Sometimes it does; it all depends on the circumstances and the people involved. Despite what happens, the appraisal of the situation, and the outcome of the assessment will be the deciding factor in the behaviour of the injured wife.

Mary and Bob were married for a few years with one child. They re-located to another state where Bob started his adulterous behaviours. Although she wanted to divorce him, she could not bring herself to do this because of her Christian values and beliefs. In fact, she was told that if she divorced Bob, she could not continue with her duties in the church. Mary, a Christian, continued with her service to the Lord and paid no attention to Bob and his infidelities. However, after Bob had a disagreement with one of his female associates, he returned home wounded. She had compassion on him and another child came. Nevertheless, Mary's forgiveness did not change Bob, and neither did the child. That marriage later ended after years of constant mental, emotional, and physical abuses. She finally came to grips with her dissonance and found some relief in alleviating the inner turmoil.

Negative dissonance

Negative dissonance exists if an individual decides that he or she had made the wrong decisions about a conflicting life event (Vander Zanden, 1988). Marriage can be one of those events especially when there is proof of infidelity.

In some situations, family members and friends warned the excited engaged future wife not to move too fast or watch how she leaps. In other cases, the woman who is anxious to be married because her "biological clock is ticking," may not seek God's direction and rather, plunge headlong into a mire of unsuspecting failure and disappointments. Occasionally, the warnings are heeded; but at other times they are not.

Depression

Although depression arise from many situations, any person might become depressed because of painful life experiences such as infidelity, the death of a loved one, diseases; substance abuse, certain types of medications, hormonal changes, or a family history of depression.

Nonetheless, whatever the reasons for depression, because it is considered to be caused by certain chemicals in the brain, it is a treatable disease. Therefore, anyone affected by this condition must seek professional help.

The signs and symptoms of depression are constant mood changes, insomnia, irritability, and loss of interest in pleasurable situations. Sudden weight and appetite loss, and restlessness are signs of depression.

In addition, the person may complain of loss of energy and fatigue, and having difficulty concentrating. Nevertheless, the condition of depression is a serious situation that needs treatment before it becomes clinical. The Blood of Jesus can heal depression, similar to all other diseases.

Therefore, it is in the interest of the woman to seek help and to admit that she has symptoms of depression, whether by self-revelation or from a trusted caring friend. Someone may notice that the woman is moody or anxious. The woman herself may complain about her sleep disorders, and this can trigger interests in a friend or relative who is knowledgeable about the symptoms of depression.

Psychological consequences resulting from infidelity will cause severe long-term problems to the wife if she does not seek professional help to support her in such a time of distress.

Chapter 32

Emotional

The emotional consequences of infidelity, similar to the psychological effects are seen in many types of behaviours such as distancing, lack of self-confidence, feelings of betrayal, shame, abandonment, worry, fear, anxiety, and embarrassment. An injured wife will also experience guilt and shame if she believes she did not contribute positively to the relationship. Those situations will make her anxious and frustrated when her husband commits adultery. There will also be times of loneliness with many recurring thoughts that will provoke her mind, causing her to spend many sleepless nights crying about her situation. Other emotional problems include the following:

Expressive Anger

Of all the emotional findings revealed in the study, anger was the most prevalent. Women have reported how angry and furious they were when they first found out about their husbands' behaviour. There were reports of both external and internal rage and hostility after the anger died down. This did not mean that the anger had disappeared. Instead, the women internalized their emotion and replaced it with the usual silent treatment while underneath the anger continues to smoulder.

Reports from Women

- *When I found out about his cheating, I could not contain myself... I met him at the door and attacked him.*
- *There was such a rage in me I felt like attacking him, but refrained from doing so.*
- *I was shocked and could not speak. I was all tensed inside, and just stared at him.*

- *I was always depressed and sometimes irritable with the children. I just cried, and cried as if I could not stop...*
- *I refused to do anything for him...I hated him and could not bear to see him.*
- *For many days, I lived in a maze only going through the motions of existence. I just could not believe it. I questioned myself and wondered what I had done.*
- *Although I was deeply hurt, I blamed myself for my husband's adultery...*
- *I had heard stories about my husband and another woman...I just did not know how to face him because he would have denied it.*
- *He was staying out late most nights and sometimes he did not come home at all, and I became suspicious...as soon as he came I bolted for him.*
- *I was bitter and always irritable with a bad temper. He stayed out of my way.*
- *He did not look at me or say anything to me; otherwise, I would have jumped on him.*
- *He compared me with his mistress. I felt like tearing him to pieces...*

Anger can be volatile and impulsive, making it become destructive. Otherwise, it can be covert if the injured woman hides her feelings. Both expressed and covert anger can sometimes be dangerous and destructive. With covert anger the pain ferments and turns into rage, and even spite against the husband.

Moreover, internalized anger has another unnoticeable side to it because it eats away self-respect, and makes the person terrified of expressing true feelings. Therefore, if the true reasons for anger are not carefully analyzed and assessed, it can be internalized with rage and fury that will hurt the individual more than when expressed in a controlled manner.

Evidently, anger that is explosive and uncontrolled will lead to severe consequences. The woman might attack her unfaithful husband in retaliation when the impact of the humiliation of the adultery becomes unbearable. Furthermore, women have destroyed every piece of their husbands' clothing upon the discovery of infidelity. Husbands themselves have confessed that they were afraid of their wives' temper. There are no winners in marital unfaithfulness.

Let me emphasize here that *the consequences of infidelity have long shadows that reaches everyone connected to the adulterer.* The women in the report were not the only ones.

Some women have suffered financially because their husbands have to take care of children resulting from infidelity or who were born before the marriage took place, but the wife was unaware of them.

Take for instance *Challis*. She reported that her husband's girlfriend would call early on a Sunday morning requesting her weekly allowance. He, in turn would speak very loudly for *Challis* to hear him arranging to take the money to the woman.

Undoubtedly, the scene was staged to torment his wife to make her miserable. Some wives have to experience these dark unexposed sides of infidelity from their cheating husbands and they suffer greatly. Therefore, no one should criticize the woman for being angry at the discovery of infidelity.

Additionally, when a woman finds out that her husband's infidelity has produced a child, should she remain calm and composed as if nothing has happened?

In some situations, the behaviour had been going on for years. Seemingly, the type of anger that proceeds after the discovery of infidelity reveals such vehemence comparable only to a volcanic eruption. It means that women can explode with unpredictable behaviours when infidelity disrupts and contaminates their lives.

Whether the infidelity is with another man or woman is of no consequence. The behaviour is still a sin and breach against the marital bond, and it will cause anger.

Presumably, it seems as if when the women became enraged that they behaved with such impact of force and fury that, had it not been for God's mercies, many of them might have done some damage to themselves or to their husbands.

It would appear that at such times they took a cursory leave of absence from their Christian obligations to vindicate themselves the only way they could, to satisfy their feelings of betrayal. *Reader, please do not judge!*

Distancing

After anger, distancing appears to be the next emotional behaviour to follow upon the discovery of infidelity. The woman will detach herself from her husband because she does not want to be part of the relationship anymore. She does this to justify her feelings of hurt, pain, and disappointment. Some women chase the men out of the bedroom, or they might remove themselves to avoid having any intimate contact with them. This action leads to intimacy avoidance because of the emotional distress experienced by the betrayal, and aversion towards the adulterous husband.

Revenge

The act of revenge is an emotive attempt at some cost or risk to impose suffering upon someone who has made another person to suffer. It is an action birthed from the emotions of shame, embarrassment, anger, and contempt (*See* Elster, 1990). Indeed, revenge can be the outcome of anger, and this behaviour can take many forms. It is all up to the personality of the individual, the state of mind, the offender, and the emotional impact from the offence.

Jealousy

The wife who remains in an adulterous relationship might become tensed with jealousy. The reason is that her husband's behaviour poses a threat to the relationship, resulting in destabilization of the marriage. Jealousy brings on feelings of insecurity that can make the wife even compare herself to the intruder into the marriage. She will find it hard to trust her husband and watches his every move.

Indifference

Women who live in unfaithful situations become indifferent towards their husbands. What seems very sad is that there are women who spiritualize the impact of the behaviour of their husbands by becoming very passive.

Some women are of the belief that the Lord is teaching them a lesson in patience. One of the reasons why women are silent to infidelity is to "keep up appearances" before the world, while in reality they and their husbands are living separate lives.

In fact, they seem to live in a state of lethargy and passivity, unaware and oblivious to the situation. The women live each day as if in a dream carrying out their tasks routinely with no motivation or enthusiasm. From sun up to sun down, life has no charm, joy, or attraction because the women have become senseless to their husbands' behaviour.

Blame

There are women who sometimes blame themselves for their husbands' adulteries. Evidently, those women in this position will bear with any types of behaviours from their unfaithful husbands because they believe they are at fault in one way or another. It is true that it takes two to break the marriage. However, no one should assume all the blame in a spiritualize manner.

Della

After a while, I became numb to the situation after living with it for so long. I accepted it because it must have been my fault since my husband has not changed, even though I have remained faithful to the Lord.

One of the situations that women who remain in an adulterous marriage will experience is emotional tension, a condition that can physically affect the woman, leading to heart and stomach problems. This condition is the result of exploitation of the woman's emotions through constant verbal or physical abuses from her husband.

These are evident in situations such as the use of swearing, put-down in the presence of others, name-calling, hitting, and manipulation for control, including any form of improper physical contact. Eventually, this condition can bear heavily upon the woman, making her feel stressed, tensed, depressed, and frustrated.

Emotional tension is the result of internal pain, and this leads to various types of other health problems, including high blood pressure, headaches and joint pain.[44] A wife can develop many health related situations when her husband actively engages in sexual relationship with several persons and this will endanger her health.[45]

---

[44] According to C.M. Narramore: "Emotional tension often play a prominent role in certain kinds of heart and circulatory disorders, especially high blood pressure – headaches, and joint muscular pain – and some allergies," *The Psychology of Counseling.* (Zondervan Publishing House, 1960): 165.

[45] B.K. Payn; K. Tanfer; O.G. Billy; and W.R. O'Grady, reported that, "sexually transmitted diseases (STDs) are a major public health problem in the United States. The writers noted that nearly 12 million persons are infected with an STD annually; approximately 43 million with viral STDs, which cannot be cured and thus infect the individual for life." *Men's Behaviour.* (Change following Infection with a Sexually Transmitted Disease," *Family Planning Perspectives,* 29, 1997): 152-157.
In a study carried out by Dolcini, et. al. the writers reported that "the percentage of newly diagnosed cases of AIDS attributed to heterosexual contact increased from 1 per cent in 1983, to approximately 6 per cent in 1992." They stated that, "individuals with more than one partners are at a greater risk of contracting the human immunodeficiency virus (HIV) and other STDs than those who have a single sexual partner." (Demographic Characteristics of Heterosexuals with Multiple Partners: The National AIDS Behaviour Surveys, *Family Planning Perspectives,* 25, (1993): 206-214.

Part V
Divorce

For she hath cast down many wounded: yea, many strong men have been slain by her. Her house is the way of hell, going down to the chambers of death (Proverbs 7:26-27).

This section covers the following topics:

- The Family Re-defined by Divorce
- Divorce Hurts Children
- Post Divorce Syndrome
- There is Life After Divorce

Chapter 33
The Family Re-defined by Divorce
[Part 1]

The issue of divorce has become commonplace that Hackney & Bernard (1990) argued that it has been "caught in the cultural values of society." They continued, "The process of divorce leaves little room for successful experiencing. Rather, it is associated with emotional trauma, loss of resources, a sense of failure, and lowered self-esteem" (p.134). These are factual outcomes from divorce, which many divorcees did not envision when they were committing adultery or carrying out their caustic diatribes against each other.

Moreover, when a woman decides that she will not forgive her unfaithful husband, and later files for divorce, usually this is because she is overwhelmed and deeply hurt. Her dreams are shattered and the entire situation seems too much to bear.

Occasionally, the rush for such a decision could be pressure from either close relatives or friends; or intense anger at that particular moment. That type of impulsive decision can make many women end up being sorry because they thought divorce would have made them happy.

Another overlooked point by those who use divorce as an alternative to heal a sick marriage is that "the adjustment to divorce is also a complex process, one that simultaneously involves the resolution of individual, couple, and family issues."[46] Those are significant situations many divorcees avoided in their decision to end the marriage by

---

[46] (Hackney & Bernard (1990, p.142).

divorce. There are hundreds of "war stories" from divorcees and their lawyers.

Therefore, everyone should take time to think about this major step in life before heading to the courts. What is so sad is that children also suffer the toxic consequences from their parents' attempt at destroying each other during the process of a divorce.

The easy access to divorce makes it the number one method for healing sick marriages and has now become a permanent fixture into the family system. What divorcees fail to see is that, while divorce may end the relationship, it really re-defines the family structure as it leaves pain, disappointment and distress in its path for many families. Children are frustrated, while mothers face financial turmoil especially if the father decides not to give support to her.

The action of divorce can be a very devastating outcome for many families. Admittedly, the presence of divorce is not new; but seemingly, when problems develop in a marriage one partner may see it as the *only* answer for resolution. For this reason, it has become a tool for the re-definition of the family system, and a major cure for sick marriages. Statistics report that from 1950-2001; the number of marriages went down from 11.1% to 8.4%. Divorce, however rose from 2.65 to 4.0% within the same period.[47]

Evidently, despite the hurts and disappointments divorce leaves in its path the rate is constantly climbing. The implication is that there might be more couples, who will seek out other arrangement for permanent relationships such as living together, rather than the Christian marriage.

If divorce takes over the family system as the only medium to heal sick marriages, then the biblical principles for marital stability will be in jeopardy. The reason is that church leaders may have difficulty

---

[47] Source: U.S. National Center for Health Statistics, *Vital Statistics of the United States*, Annual; and *National Vital Statistics*. From *Reports (NVSR)* (formerly *Monthly Vital Statistics Report*); and unpublished data. Vital Statistics #59 U.S. Census Bureau, Statistical Abstract of the United States: 2002. Divorce rates exclude data for California, Colorado, Indiana, and Louisiana.

getting their members to adhere to those traditional beliefs, once held sacred to Christianity.

Moreover, the situation is getting even more critical since nowadays leaders from all strata of society have been involved in behaviours that led to extra-marital affairs which, in some cases have resulted into divorces.

It appears that when the relationship begins to lose the novelty and attractiveness rather than seek the help of professional counseling a couple or at least one partner lets the relationship freeze to death. Why destroy a relationship if there is faith in God to heal and restore the marriage? Is there no other alternative for sick marriages?

For the Christian, divorce should not be the answer when problems arise in the marriage. Instead, it should be the exception. Jesus told the disciples, *"Moses because of the hardness of your hearts suffered* [permitted] *you to put away your wives: but from the beginning it was not so"* (Matthew 19:8).

Obviously when one partner becomes hard and unforgiving, there will be the temptation for taking the route of divorce. The sin of unforgiveness will certainly hold the marriage in bondage because the enemy has infiltrated the relationship blocking all access for communication and harmony.

Consequently, once the devil snatches an opportunity to *sow* the seed of discord, *watered* by doubts, and *fertilized* by an unforgiving spirit, there is little hope left for reconciliation without God's direct intervention. The devil seizes the opportunity to *magnify* faults as he highlights the weaknesses of a wrongdoer.

For instance, even when someone admits to the sin of adultery, should any person take God's place and condemn that person without hearing from the individual, or should there be space for mercy? Furthermore, every marriage will have some types of faults because of the sinful nature of the human heart.

Conceivably, any marriage will, and can end in divorce if the partners use their natural inclinations as the basis for choosing each other for a lifetime relationship. In some situations partners are unequally yoked, and this often causes problems.

To be unequally yoked involves many situations. For example, it could be that one person is a Christian and the other is not. During courtship, it is easy to tell each other "we will take care of our problems later," but after the honeymoon ends, so do many of those promises. Those promises go underground.

Continues in the next Chapter

Chapter 34
The Family Re-defined by Divorce
[Part 2]

Women of Faith

Despite the increase in divorces, there are women with strong moral and religious objections toward taking this action to heal problems in their marriage. Those persons are not only Christians, but some are people who do not practice Christianity. One could describe them as "women of faith who are willing to trust God to heal the sin of adultery in their marriages.

In some cases, the women try to hold on to those marital vows made by their husbands to love, honour, and protect them. Unfortunately, those pledges seem very hollow when their husbands turn to adulterous behaviours. However, adultery does not stop women who are willing to take the risk that their husbands will change from those behaviours. I have heard women say, "I leave it up to the Lord."

The Scriptures declare that with God *all* things are possible. Consequently, if the hurt wife truly believes those words and relies on God's promises, her hope is that someday deliverance will come, because God does not fail, nor can He lie. In fact, waiting on God is a demonstration of faith and trust in His unfailing promises. Understandably, this action requires courage, trust, and faith.

Surely, you might say, "Must I wait forever?" Only God knows how long. However, the woman who purposes in her heart that she will wait for God to act on her behalf will never be sorry so long as she does whatever He directs her to do. It is possible that some marriages will eventually end in divorce. Still, divorce should only be a last resort.

Moral Decadence

I ask, "Can this millennium re-direct the immoral social trend and set a pattern for better lifestyles or is society sliding deeper into the abyss of moral decay?" Undoubtedly, if we fail to acknowledge God in our daily lives, and instead proclaim our right to do what we want, then there is little hope of ever seeing a trace of the standards grandparents embraced generations ago.

The selfish desires of people have changed the moral fabric of society to satisfy their own lusts, passions, self-centeredness, desires, greed, lifestyles, and sinful nature? Is divorce is the *only* answer for a sick marriage? This should be the exception, rather than the rule.

It is reasonable to state, that the sophistication of technology and science has made education easily obtainable. It has become more affordable and reachable to most people, so that learners can remain at home and receive training for almost any career.

With this in mind women may no longer make the effort to remain in a sick marriage to maintain their financial status. They will prepare themselves in order to find employment positions that will keep them in their previous financial state before divorce. Actually, some women have emerged from divorce better off than when they depended on their husbands. Consequently, divorces will increase and the downward spiral will continue.

The Position of the Church

Nevertheless, can the church point a finger at the world when infidelity, divorce, and separation have become common events, from the pulpit to the pew? What then is the Christian church doing to arrest the precipitous decline of spiritual and moral values for this, and the next generation? Is divorce the answer? Is homosexuality the answer? What is the answer? These are critical issues in the world today, and surely the church must acknowledge that it has failed in many ways. It is clear that society has made its statement that it does not want God into its culture. What has the church done to correct this situation? Has the Word of God lost its power? Emphatically No!

However, while it may seem easy to place blame on the failure of the church, we must consider the facts of the church's situation. In many places, leaders no longer have the freedom to speak about issues as they once did. In many churches, the trend is that anything that seems antisocial [politically incorrect] must not be spoken even from the pulpits. Therefore, many ministers only stick to the mission of saving souls; and avoid controversial issues to keep the peace.

Furthermore, since some denominations are winking at the flimsy reasons for divorce this behaviour will become the "quick fix" for sick marriages in the church. Let me say that divorce is not always the answer because it weakens the structure of the family. Children get hurt, spouses get hurt, and many more people get hurt. Besides, divorce has long-lasting results.

In some families, repetitive divorces seem to have been the central factor for some generational situations because it follows from one generation to the next.

The Sex Concept

Continuing, one of the reasons why divorce ends some marriages is because sex was the foundation for the marriage, and it is used as a weapon or exchange to gain favours in the relationship. There comes a time when that enticement loses its glow causing the other partner to wander into new adventures and exploits.

Many couples do not seem to understand that the act of sex is a demonstration of love, and for procreation. Couples should not use it to precede a marriage, or as a tool against the other when things go wrong. To do this is to be in disobedience of God's Word, while the behaviour will place a wedge into the marital relationship. In addition, sex should not be the reason for getting married; otherwise it would have lost the real value placed upon it by God.

Divorce and Re-Marriage

The issue of divorce and re-marriage is debatable. Many churches do not uphold this practice because the belief is that the union must remain intact. The teaching is that only death of one of the spouses can end the marriage after consummation, no matter who was at fault.

Moreover, those churches are extremely inflexible, so that the minister will not marry a divorced member. In fact, the individual's membership is terminated because of the divorce, and of course the re-marriage. I will not enter into discussion with this aspect of marital issue since the focus of the chapter is on divorce. However, there are justifiable circumstances when a divorce will sometimes be advisable.

While it is true that the Mosaic Law supports divorce (*See* Deuteronomy 24:1), Jesus spoke strongly against such a method stating, "*Moses, because of the hardness of your hearts suffered you to put away your wives: but from the beginning it was not so*" (Matthew 19:8). Still, despite Moses' Law, divorce was not encouraged on the grounds of false accusations (*See* Deuteronomy 22:18, 19).

Surprisingly, in this age and in some denominations, if a reverend has been divorced such person can re-marry, maybe even more than once. However, under the Mosaic Law, a priest was forbidden to marry a divorced woman (Leviticus 21:14).

Again, every case is different and I am not here to judge anyone. I am only stating observations. Anyway, Jesus' teachings on divorce were clear, "*But I say unto you, that whosoever shall put away his wife, saving for the cause of fornication, causes her to commit adultery*" (Matthew 5:32; 19:9). Since in earlier times the basis for divorce was for any slight misdemeanour by a wife, Jesus' teachings represent grace, tolerance, and forgiveness, thus regulating the practice of divorce.

The Bible teaches that the only time divorce is permissible is in the case of adultery. Moreover, Paul emphasized that when there are problems in the relationship the couple should remain together; but if one of them departs, the other partner should try to reconcile (*See* I Corinthians 7: 1-16, 39).

Nevertheless, let everyone take this caveat in mind that the allurement of divorce has far-reaching consequences that touches everyone in the family. The divorced spouse is often alone, and in some cases financially insecure. Children are separated from one parent, and forced to choose sides.

Furthermore, in a disastrous divorce enemies are created on both sides of the family as well as between the spouses. Incredibly, but some divorcees will admit that they are the best of friends now that they are not in close proximity of each other. I cannot understand the reason nor do I have an answer. Maybe social science researchers could use this as a topic for exploration.

Consequently, unless family members decide to make proper choices and live a life that is moral and godly, it is possible for the divorce trend to continue unabated.

In conclusion, the path of divorce is not the answer to all problems that develop in a marriage. In the Word of God we read that God hates divorce, but stressed oneness in the marital relationship. This explains why a man leaves his father and mother and is joined to his wife, and the two are united into one-flesh (*See* Genesis 2:24).

Let us not forget that whatever affects the family will affect the community, and ultimately the society. It only takes one spark to get a fire going. Think about it!

Chapter 35

Divorce Hurts Children

For some children, the divorce of their parents can be the most painful experience, especially if a choice has to be made between the parents for custody. Children do suffer and some of them carry their feelings into adulthood.

Moreover, when parents divorce they do not seem to consider their children and the effect of the change on their lives unless it is to the advantage of both or one of them. Seemingly, each parent is planning to meet personal needs and convenience rather than the benefit and support the child/children.

In some situations, a child may have to travel from one state to the next to spend a little quality time with a parent, and then only to return to the custodial parent. Those types of arrangements give the children an unstable emotional health. This was not God's plan for a healthy family life.

Undoubtedly, the greatest impact divorce has on a child is the decision to choose one parent over the other for residence. Surely, this places a great burden on their young shoulders.

What makes matters worse is when the divorce was a difficult and bitter one and parents squabble in the presence of those impressionable young hearts.

Parents, divorce is hurting your children. Even if you cannot agree with each other, hate one another to the core if you must, but please do not give your children an inkling of your bad feelings towards each other. It is not fair to them. They did not marry you. You chose each other. When parents behave disrespectfully before children, the idea is that they are inconvenience rather blessings to them. They may not verbalize, but their very actions communicate those idea.

For example "I can't keep him because I only have a one bedroom apartment." "I have to go to school at nights and cannot afford a baby-sitter." These are only some of the lava which spews from the mouths of parents in the presence of their children when a divorce takes place. My suggestion is that you do your arguing away from them and not in their presence. Therefore, do not let the fall-out of your toxic emotional assault fall upon your children.

Before I leave this spot, I must make another point. There are parents who vie for the spotlight against each other to impress the children concerning which of the two of them is better. This is a deceptive and foolish behaviour.

Do you really think the children do not know what you are doing, especially if they are old enough to understand? In another situation, there are parents who lie on each other to gain the support of a child against the other parent. This behaviour is despicable.

Parents, even if one of you committed adultery, do not destroy the other before the children. You are still a parent whom the child loves. Mothers are guilty of this behaviour because they use their hurt and hatred after their husband's adultery as a weapon to destroy the relationship between that child and the father. Even if you did not commit adultery, are you any better than the adulterer who committed such sin? I hardly think so.

Parents, if you want your children to grow up loving and respecting you, then you must continue to show respect and regard for each other, particularly in their presence. In any case, you will be much happier and emotionally healthier. Do not speak negatively about each other to deceive the children about your ex's character. Because a divorce occurs does not mean that life is over.

Chapter 36

Post Divorce Syndrome

Ultimately, there are no winners in a divorce proceeding because everyone involved has lost something of value or someone because each partner loses each other, and children lose the proximity of one parent in the home. Divorce opens up a canister of worms that extends for years.

It is even more devastating when the divorce was a disastrous one. The aftermath covers custody, support, graduations, marriages, births, and deaths. There is emotional and psychological pain, shame, and embarrassment to some individuals. It is disappointing to observe partners, who once *deeply* loved each other, how they can become bitter enemies to the point of hatred after a divorce.

However, the experience of divorce is extremely painful for some ex-wives. I wonder if the financial loss is as painful as the loneliness, disappointment, remorse, regret, loss, emotional pain, and misery. It is true that many couples do not face the destructive fall-out of post divorce syndromes. Still, some individuals do, and this memory can leave a lasting impression.

- *When I left the courtroom, I felt as though I had been stripped, and laid bare.*
- *Not many people know that I had divorced my husband.*
- *I still feel the shame and embarrassment of being divorced.*
- *I did not want a divorce because of my Christian faith, but the women would call the house and insult me...*
- *I just could not stand it anymore along with the physical and emotional abuses from my husband, so I divorced him.*

Although a husband might still pay alimony in some cases, and help with child support and rearing, many women face financial burdens after a divorce. One woman complained about the loss of financial security.

When my husband and I were together, since he earned more than I did, he paid most of the bills. After the divorce, I found myself having to pay all those bills by myself while I take care of other things and help with the financial needs of the children.

Women have even experienced ostracism from some church members.

- *My pastor told me if I divorced my husband, I would not be allowed to continue my duties in the church.*
- *I have seen times when members would treat me as if I had committed a crime, even though they knew what I endured with my husband.*

Emotional loneliness is a side effect of divorce, and for this reason, many divorcees seek out new romantic exploits. Others will become recluse and cut themselves off from social activities, friends and loved ones. I would not advise either of the two, although it is normal for a time of healing and dealing with the grief of loss to take place after the trauma of divorce. In many cases, the damage is great, making the repair to the emotions a difficult process.

Physical and emotional loneliness have a great impact on the divorcee because there is a vacant space in the home, and in the life of the individual. The house suddenly becomes extremely large and empty, even when there are children around.

While divorce may seem fanciful with its freedom of an offending partner, it has some very painful moments. Let no one underestimate the overwhelming impact of divorce and the loneliness that follows.

- *I suddenly felt alone and just did not know what to do with myself.*
- *It was as if the whole world was closing in upon me.*
- *I missed my husband just being there even though he was unfaithful to me.*
- *Just knowing that a man was coming into the house at night was satisfying to me.*
- *I would have stayed with him despite his behaviour, but he insisted on having a divorce so I went ahead with it. If I could have turned back the clock, I would not have gone through with the divorce...I would have waited it out...*

The burden of loneliness after a divorce is not similar to that of the widow whose husband has died. The difference is that the dead husband is 'gone' while the living ex-husband is still alive to share children and life events, even though the marriage itself is dead.

For the woman who decides to remain unmarried, the very thought of her husband living with or married to another woman is like rubbing salt into the wounds after the divorce. She might say that this does not matter to her, but I hardly believe that many women are being truthful to themselves. How do they deal with the knowledge that he is making love to someone else?

Sometimes the church family, of which the woman is a part, often forgets her or treats her with a cold shoulder. Many will say, "Oh, I don't want to interfere, and furthermore, I don't know what to say." "She was not spiritual enough." "She *must* have seen it coming." "The poor dear, she looks so sad." Otherwise, some will ask questions, and then spread the answers like wild fire. When it reaches the woman, it tears her into small pieces hurting her all over again.

Indeed, there are some busybodies in churches I will call "well-intentioned-empathizers," similar to Job's friends. It is no surprise that women remain silent about infidelity and divorce. In some cases, the divorced woman loses her married "friends" because they are afraid she might take away their husbands. This is true. It does happen.

- *I don't ever hear when there is an event outside of the church until after the fact.*
- *Someone might say, "I went to a play..." or "I went to a banquet at..." Very rarely do I receive an invitation to go anywhere.*
- *Some wives are suspicious of me when I am around their husbands. It is awful facing such situations.*
- *I get some horrible looks from married women if their husbands barely come near me to shake my hand or to talk with me.*

There is a particular new trend that women with young children who seek divorce should pay attention before making such a decision. Some husbands may run away to avoid paying child support. They may even leave one state for another and that money will accumulate until the law catches up with them. However, men are getting more vicious and subtle.

166

Instead of running away or having their wages garnished to pay child support they are now leaving their jobs and not looking for any other, if only to avoid paying that money. It stands to reason. If they are not working, they can spite the wife whom they consider to be greedy and thus hurt their children. Women, if you *must* divorce, make sure you can survive without your ex-husband's income as a supplement. [JIC] *Just in case!*

Finally, it does not make sense divorcing and then tying up your life with two and three jobs. This is indeed folly and adding more pain to the injuries of infidelity and divorce. Children do grow up and after a while, that man's behaviour no longer has the same impact as it did when you first discovered his adultery.

Furthermore, time does heal wounds! Obviously, women who can hold on to the marriage until children go to college are doing the right thing. It makes sense.

Still, if you are going to remain in the marriage, do not make yourself a nuisance with hatred and malice or chart out a life of unhappiness to get sympathy. You will have to be strong and courageous with the help of the Lord.

Think twice [no], many times over before taking the route to the divorce lawyer.

Chapter 37

There is Life after Divorce and Infidelity

Undeniably, divorce has many disappointments and setbacks for some divorcees; yet it is possible to begin life again in terms of finance, emotions, and self-confidence. However, the divorcee should not allow the past to dictate what the future might, or could be. A general assessment of one's talents, aims, and future goals are important.

Many women have been able to pick themselves up and start life all over again. The fact that the marriage has failed does not mean that *they* have failed. On the contrary, a failed marriage occurred because two people had differences that they were unable to deal with or resolve.

What I am pointing out is that after divorce it is pointless trying to gather up the spilt milk or to blame the adulterer for his dishonest conduct or unfaithfulness to the marriage. Also, when the door is closed, *stop knocking;* gather some dignity, and move on with your life.

Most importantly, get hold of your thoughts and do not cogitate over past likes and dislikes. Do not spend endless time crying and fretting over your losses. You have shed enough tears over the marriage already. Why manufacture more? There will be no need for them. Your husband is gone, and the marriage is over, take some time for grief; but do not spend the rest of your life getting over your losses.

Do not drown yourself into a pool of sorrow. Do not rent an apartment in the city of self-pity. When you do that, you will become dried and withered, similar to a prune with channels of misery coursing down your face. This will make you look graceless and older than your years.

Anyway, so what if your husband and you are divorced? Does this stop you from living? Do not give up on your life because of divorce or rejection from the person you *thought* would have been a lifetime partner. The fact of the matter is that *not all marriages last*, and *all spouses are not faithful*.

Unquestionably, divorce is a life-changing event often overwhelming, but anyone can overcome this experience. Therefore, the divorcee should not become a prisoner to this disappointing life-event because it has disrupted and changed personal plans.

It is better to seek for wholesome alternatives that will give enjoyment, and fill the void of loss. Furthermore, the individual should give God the chance to heal those damaged emotions.

If you are a divorcee who is still clutching yesterday's pleasant memories wishing you could re-live the past, it is time to get rid of those expectations of waiting for your husband to return to you. What will you do if he never comes back?

If you must wait, then while you are waiting enjoy your children, your life, your church, your social organization, or join a support group. If you do not have one, find one, but get *connected!*

The Bible states: "*A man that has friends must show himself friendly...*"[48] Do not give up on life because it will not come running after you. The rest of your life is up to you. If you cut yourself off from people and crawl into a hole because you have lost the love of your life, this will not help you. It is the first rung down the spiral staircase of emotional destruction.

Persons in this situation use substances to ease the pain of emotional blackmail. It is a form of emotional blackmail because the devil is telling the individual that self-destruction will cause the other person to return. Furthermore, the use of substances to heal your emotions will bring you under their control and make you think that you cannot live

---

[48] Proverbs 18:24b

without another pill, drink, smoke, and so on.

Bear in mind that substances are not lasting friends to the hurting. Do not hold your breath! Life is not that generous, at least not for most people. It is better to put your trust in God (Proverbs 3:5, 6) who will not fail you.

There is life after divorce, but it is up to the divorcee to find it in God, and allow Him to take control by leading and guiding her in the way He chooses. She should build a strong and intimate relationship with the Lord Who will be there when she is feeling sad and all alone. He is the only one who can heal her broken heart.

Additionally, loneliness should not become a shelter in which to hide. That is another emotional blackmail from the devil. The reason is that loneliness is one of the negative emotions that will make a divorcee behave in ways that she might never have thought of behaving before. Nothing is wrong if one feels alone, it is normal because we are all social beings requiring companionship and love.

Managing Loneliness

If the individual does not fill the vacuum of loneliness with the right thoughts that will lead to a proactive response, it can spell disaster. It is therefore important for the divorced person to accept the change and allow God to help soothe the emotional hurts and pains.

Earlier I talked about being connected. Do not stop there, get *involved!* Also, do not be a third "person" with another couple even though they are sometimes necessary and important, but only in an emergency. *Get a life for yourself!* Aim to be more than a third "person." This will make you look desperate. Be a part of, and get involved with interesting activities.

What do you like to do? What gives you the most enjoyment out of life? Who are the people you like to be around you? Where do you like to go? What is going on in your community, or church? Do not merely exist; *live* and enjoy your life. Be thankful that you are still able to see, hear, do, and go. Do not take the necessary physical independence of life for granted. Instead, use them to their fullest and be thankful that you are still alive and can do things for yourself.

Be appreciative and thankful to God every day of your life. Do not drown yourself into the turbulent murky sea of self-pity. Give thanks that the situation did not make you lose your sanity, or even your life.

Moreover, be thankful that you had those years with him, especially if this was a first marriage and you had the children, I mean think about it, you are the mother of the children. What if he is gone? *Live*, and celebrate life! Just *live* and be thankful that you are still whole and can think for yourself.

In addition, change your appearance if you need to do so. Get a new hairdo, wardrobe, manicure, pedicure, body massage; a complete makeover! Treat yourself for a change and stop fretting about a man who is gone out of your life. Go on a cruise! Join a gym and lose some weight. Put a twinkle in your eye, and a spring in your step. Move on with your life and give your "friends" something to gossip about you. Stay focussed; take care of yourself because no else will do it for you.

Do not give up! Some women are in hiding from their husbands and others have died. Practice thinking good wholesome thoughts; read good, informative books that are inspiring and enlightening. Learn to laugh at silly things and do not be so serious, harsh, and stern with yourself.

When was the last time you had a good laugh from the diaphragm upward? I mean a *good, strong,* and *hearty belly* laugh that gives you the shakes. Stop stretching your lips, [smirking with the stiff upper lip] and begin to laugh at the funny sides of life, it will be very beneficial for you.[49] Stop being so sad and enjoy the beauties of life. Pause and smell the roses, paying careful attention to the intricacies of the petals.

---

[49] Proverbs 17:22 "*A merry heart doeth good like a medicine: but a broken spirit drieth the bones.*"

Look at the way the Great Artist painted those lovely flowers no artist can perfectly duplicate.

Take some time to admire a beautiful baby, sunrise, sunset, and listen to the singing of birds. Go for walks and appreciate the season. Take a long drive, or go to the beach. Pamper yourself with a long luxurious candlelight bubble bath. Love yourself for a change. You have the rest of your life to live, so live it with enjoyment. Also, spend quality time in the Word and in prayer with the Lord while you are regaining yourself. If you must reminisce, do not dwell on the negatives. Let them be migratory storm clouds. If the rain must fall, let it!

Here are some questions to answer before going into a new relationship:
- What do you want for yourself out of this relationship?
- What will you do to accomplish your desire?
- What changes do you need to make, for the new relationship to be better?
- How willing are you to adapt?
- Are you willing to make concessions?
- What are your weaknesses and strengths?
- What are the things you hate in yourself, and others?
- What makes you angry; happy or sad; cry or laugh?
- What do you want from the other person?

<u>Whatever you do, get the bitterness out of your system</u>.
Purge yourself and renew your mind about life!
Avoid harbouring toxins of guilt, hatred, malice, revenge,
animosities, resentments, hostilities, and grudges.
Let go, and let God!

======

You Are Special

Think of yourself as the most beautiful rose in the
garden;
The calm ripple in the river;
The soft wave of the sea;
Your favourite colour in the rainbow;
The delicate sunrise in the east;
The beautiful sunset in the west;
The soft gentle dew on the grass;
The unique snowflake that gently falls to the ground.
You are the most beautiful person created by God.
You are special,
Because God created you different from everyone else.

Chapter 38

You Made the Decision to Remain

I now turn to those women who have made the decision to remain with their unfaithful husbands. Unless you are willing to forgive the behaviour and move on with your life, it would be foolhardy to remain only for the sake of victimizing your husband. I did say forgive. This does not mean that you have condoned his infidelities.

On the contrary, what it means is that you are taking control of *your* life and not using *his* behaviour as an excuse to keep you in bondage by harbouring a grudge. You are the only one who will be carrying that baggage. It is foolish to remain in a marriage that only causes pain and make you bitter and miserable. If you remain, then let it be for a good reason that you are comfortable with.

In William Shakespeare's play *A Midsummer Night's Dream*, we see a lover's quadrangle. Puck, one of the conspirator's in this comedy uttered these famous words *"Lord, what fools we mortals be!"*[50] It is indeed foolish to remain in a situation that has no meaning, other than to bring heartache and pain to everyone, mainly to yourself. Apparently, the woman who bears a lifetime grudge against her husband, and who tries to hurt him is portraying someone who has had her heart torn out by a serpent's claws.

Solomon said:

> I see more cruel than death the woman, whose heart is snares and nets, and her hands as bands: whoso pleases God will escape from her; but the sinner shall be taken by her.[51]

---

[50] From William Shakespeare: The Complete Works, *A Midsummer Night's Dream, Act III, Scene II*, (Dorset Press, 1988), p. 290
[51] Ecclesiastes 7:26

Evidently, the man who is faithful to his wife has a better chance of escaping such a woman. Furthermore, one of the results of revenge is generational curse. Therefore, the woman who cherishes factors of hatred, malice, and resentment towards her unfaithful husband is passing her negative behaviours down to her children and grandchildren.

Therefore, if you care for yourself and want to leave a legacy of love and emotional health to the next generation, learn to forgive and move on with your life. You may leave millions of dollars behind you, but if your curse follows, it will continue until someone gets wise and breaks it.

Undeniably, infidelity is destructive and divorce breaks up the family. Still, when those situations occur a woman should not end her life by living in miscry. To do so would be suicidal. It is like someone who frequently tries to take his or her life, but does not succeed because that person may only be seeking for attention.

Why hurt own self? Can you blame your husband for the rest of your life? Can you even blame him for your unhappiness? Life is what *you* make it. Therefore, it is up to *you* to find some type of peace after infidelity, or even divorce.

For those women who are living in a marriage that is like an albatross around your necks, stop being so cruel to yourself. It is time to re-assess the reasons for your actions. Reflect on your decision. If you are happy, then make sure that you are also comfortable with the arrangement. It makes no sense living in a situation that causes you endless grief and pain.

Tips For Keeping Your Marriage Safe

- Take time to be with each other. Go for walks together.
- Set up surprise outings and dates for just the two of you.
- Turn off the phone and plan a candlelight dinner.
- Take weekend vacations together.
- Make every effort to please each other.
- Do not take quarrels to the bedroom or keep overnight.
- Deal with your differences early so that they do not turn into battles/war.
- Admire each other and your children.
- Learn to laugh at each other, and with each other.
- Learn to listen even when neither of you is talking.
- Pay attention to body languages; they tell more than words.
- Love each other unconditionally. Respect each other.
- Make every effort to keep out intruders.
- Talk over problems and learn to resolve them together.
- Seek outside help if need be.
- Learn to relax to avoid stress and tension.
- Pray and read the Word of God together, and often.
- Attend church regularly; the two of you and in the same car if possible.
- Allow each other your individuality, but live in oneness the way God intended.
- Practice healthy eating habits, thoughts, and attitudes.
- Be sensitive to each other – do not assume or judge.
- Be together, often. Sometimes turn off the lights to avoid busybodies.
- Some "friends" are not worth a phone call – *drop them.*

Part VI

Conflict

The chapters in this section discuss the *Relationship of Interpersonal Conflict and Infidelity.*

Whether therefore ye eat, or drink, or whatsoever ye do, do all to the glory of God (1 Corinthians 10:31, KJV)

Follow peace with all men, and holiness, without which no man shall see the Lord: Looking diligently lest any man fall of the grace of God; lest any root of bitterness springing up trouble you, and thereby many be defiled (Hebrews 12:14 - 15)

This Section includes the following:

- Some Features about Conflict
- Interpersonal Conflict and Infidelity
- The Biblical Perspectives on Marital Problems
- Some Reasons for Marital Conflicts
- Reactions to Problems
- Resolving Marital Interpersonal Conflicts
- Forgiveness and Infidelity

Chapter 39

Some Features about Conflict

Conflict is either interpersonal, or intra-psychic in nature. Intra-psychic conflict occurs in the mind of the individual through the thought pattern, while interpersonal conflict is the interaction between individuals.

When there is a break in the marital relationship, these two variables will interface with each other through the thinking process and emotions, resulting in feelings that lead to negative attitudes and behaviours. Obviously, three domains are at work in a given situation: cognitive [*thoughts*], affective [*emotions*], and behavioural [*active display of expressions*].

Besides, when conflict occurs in any relationship, it may be destructive or constructive. However, conflict in and of itself is not destructive; rather it is the way the disputants deal with the issues that will result in conflict escalation.

For example, if the husband is remorseful, the wife may grudgingly forgive him. Still, the husband might be militant and disrespectful with the idea that he is a man and is entitled to do what he wants with this life and money. This is where the situation gets out of control and someone ends up being hurt.

Types of Conflict

Destructive Conflict

Research suggests that interpersonal conflict can be a source of benefit with proper handling. Nonetheless, any type of conflict has the tendency to become volatile and destructive if there are communication problems in the relationship. Destructive conflict includes: failing to acknowledge the problem, withdrawal, ignoring the significance of conflict, spiritualization, keeping score, attacking the person instead of the problem, blaming someone else, desiring to win at any cost, and buying a way out.[52] Some of those factors were also emerging themes in the data for the research carried out by this writer.

Constructive Conflict

When marital conflict occurs, it can be a positive factor if it leads to change that will improve communication and interpersonal relationship. Therefore, constructive conflict management will allow the couple to reveal feelings to each other without rancour or fear as they seek for ways to bring resolution to those differences. Moreover, the discussion will reveal hidden problems in the relationship. Essentially, there must be an analysis of the situations that precipitate any disagreement, before resolution can take place. It is also very important to separate the issues from each other and avoid personal attacks.

Integrative

If the couple is seeking for common ground, they will use integrative tactics[53] of trust and intimacy, rather than focus on the issues. This means that they will take time to discuss the problems to find ways for resolution, instead of causing those situations to escalate. Therefore, even after an affair has occurred, if the two people decide to seek help so that they can understand underlying causes, there is every hope for healing for the marriage. One must understand that divorce is not always the answer to infidelity.

Distributive

This is the opposite of integrative because it results in competitiveness, threats, and sarcasm that may only lead to further breakdown in the relationship, even if one wins the argument.[54] When an injured partner

---

[52] McDowell, (1993)
[53] S. Duck, *Understanding Relationships*. (The Guildford Press, 1991).
[54] Ibid, Duck

adopts this strategy, that individual is acting selfishly, especially if there was no discussion. The act of adultery is a breach to the commitment of marriage. Still, can we assign blame to only one person? Since there are two individuals in the relationship, one can assume that each contributed to the problems that exist between them. Frequently, it seems so much easier to show contempt for the offender, rather than try to secure healing and reconciliation.

Conflict Resolution Styles

Accommodating

Despite the hurts and embarrassment to her and the family, a wife may not display any opposition to her husband's infidelities. Instead, she struggles with her emotions and avoid expressing them. Some wives in this situation will argue that, *"He takes care of the home, that's all that matters."* This is an example of accommodating and being cooperative about a situation that causes emotional and psychological discomforts. Besides, if by ignoring the husband's adultery will give the woman a sense of peace, then it is her choice, her way of coping with the behaviour in order to have some type of consolation and peaceful stability.

Compromising

In another situation where a husband stays away for long periods and only returns home occasionally, his wife might compromise this behaviour by making demands on her husband, if only to satisfy some of her needs.

For example, she will ignore his behaviour, and negotiate with him to obtain whatever she requires, and ensure that he does not reduce his support to the home. Most wives in such a situation are either grandmothers or just could not careless what their husbands do. They only want their husbands to leave them alone, but still take care of them financially.

Obviously, accommodating and compromising unfaithfulness are detrimental to the marital relationship because they do not resolve interpersonal conflicts.

Those types of conflict management styles serve only as temporary trade-offs, and tit-for-tat. They are only momentary peace offerings, but they do not stop adultery. Moreover, those behaviours may only lower the self-esteem of the injured wife and will later cause feelings of frustration and shame.

Competitiveness

In this situation, the wife thinks only of her interests, and tries to get even with the husband by using various tactics to compensate her for his wrong doings. Further, she may turn this to her advantage and become unreasonable by asking her husband for all kinds of things to keep her quiet if he does not want the situation to be known by others. The competitive approach can also be compromising at times or even accommodating depending on the mood of the woman. Adultery is a dangerous game to play depending on who swings the pendulum.

Collaborative

This is the cooperative approach when the injured wife decides to put her hurts aside in an attempt to work out the problems with outside help. With this method, both the wife and husband are willing to face the situation together to save the marriage with the use of open discussions, and honesty.

Many couples have been able to overcome adultery despite its destructive nature because the desire is for a win/win outcome. However, with lose/win; and win/lose styles, only one person wins. In any case, in a divorce no one wins, and that can be described as the lose/lose style for managing marital conflict.

People will use many types of approaches to resolve conflicts. Even so, the success of marital conflict management depends on the cooperation of both husband and wife. It is important that the couple have a strong motivation to build the relationship and is committed to the demands of its maintenance. A successful marital relationship is a high maintenance undertaking for all married couples.

Admittedly, every marriage will experience conflicts because they are a part of life. Nevertheless, no wife should live in mental and or emotional bondage resulting from the cruelty and insensitive behaviour of her husband. Likewise methods of accommodating, compromising or being competitive only lower the self-worth and values of an individual. They are not positive responses to interpersonal conflict.

Peace should be pursued at all times, but it must be won with the right tools. Still, every situation is different and each person must know what is best for her in order to have peace of mind and some kind of stability in the relationship.

Naturally, in the world nations use guns and other means to obtain peace. However, in the Body of Jesus Christ, there are other methods for securing peace with God and man. Clearly, if spouses purpose in their hearts to maintain faith, honesty, loyalty, and integrity in the relationship, there will be no reason to experience the Betrayal of Sacred Trust.

Nevertheless, "it cannot be over-emphasized that conflict is an everyday occurrence in interpersonal relationships."[55] Therefore, it is not unique to marriage. For this reason, couples must first acknowledge problems in the marriage, and be willing to discuss them rather than avoid, deny, or pretend they do not exist.

---

[55] Zueschner, R. 1997

Chapter 40

Interpersonal Conflict and Infidelity

Interpersonal conflict is a major factor for marital instability, but common to all human relationships. The reason is that people interact with each other through action, verbal and non-verbal communication. What is most important of communication however, is how the message that is sent is received, rather than how it was sent. The reason is that communication with others means that there should be sensitivity and respect for personal feelings.

Therefore, an adulterer is making a statement to his wife without even a spoken word. His actions are communicative signals expressing his value to the relationship. In such a situation, the atmosphere is electric with hostilities, animosities, sadness, and misery. Children become restless and concerned because there is obstruction in the natural state of affairs in the home. One cannot overlook the fact that the exposure of adultery will without doubt result in interpersonal conflicts because there has been a rupture in the relationship.

Regarding interpersonal relationship, there are writers who are of the opinion that interpersonal conflict is both inevitable in human relationships, but intrinsically neutral in nature.[56] When conflicts occur it is true that they can be neutral, but even the neutral ones can escalate and cause problems. People often behave according to their moods, the season, type of weather, and the way life seems to be treating them. On a given day when someone is feeling sad, even the slightest offense can become magnanimous.

---

[56] Scheiner and Wolper, 1996

Another writer argued that not all conflicts are neutral or beneficial.[57] The reason is that conflict can arise out of greed and selfish desires which are sinful to the life of the Christian. For example, some women have to be at every sale, or they have to be in all the latest fashions. This may be all right when the couple can afford to spend the money for those purchases. However, in a financial distress this can create the most problems in a marriage if that woman cannot spend as she accustom.

Consequently, if one partner's motive for marrying is with an attitude of "what's in it for me", the lack of finance will be the decisive factor for breaking the covenant. However, in the case of a wife, if that person accomplishes her desires, obviously there will be reasons to remain; but when there are financial disappointments the marriage may suffer.

In such a situation, the wife can become moody and irritable when there are financial problems. In fact, this seems to be one of the major problems for marital breakdowns. Evidently, the main interest in such a marriage was for selfish reasons and not for permanence and happiness. There are also those who marry for social purposes, and for cultural satisfaction. In the latter, this may be an arranged marriage to join families together. In any of those cases, after a while those persons may find that they are not compatible, and this will result in interpersonal conflicts.

Another writer noted that conflicts are inevitable because of differences in the background of individuals, viewpoints, emotions, and culture, which for example, partners bring into their marriage.[58] There can be no dispute about this example because they are factual.

Still, Maloney (1995) added that conflicts are desperate feelings of threats to one's self-esteem that can lead to drastic acts of self-defense.

---

[57] K. Sande, *The Peacemaker: A Biblical Guide to Resolving Personal Conflict.* 2nd ed. (Baker Books, 1997).
[58] McDowell, 1993

Indeed, when a wife finds out that her husband has been unfaithful, in most cases there is the urge for some type of verbal, emotional, or physical response to this assault on the relationship.

The reason is that the woman suffered an emotional injury to her sense of worth either through shame or embarrassment from her husband's adultery resulting in feelings of discomfort. Besides, the emotional injuries of infidelity cause genuine feelings of pain, sorrow, and anguish. It is true that not all wives behave with anger and outbursts of emotions, but they seem to be the exception.

Sturgis (1995) further noted that conflict does not imply hostility, but that it may escalate into hostile confrontation. Naturally, infidelity will make the patterns of communication become forced, and the whole atmosphere charged with anger and bitterness, especially from the injured wife.

There are wives who will testify that they have confronted their husband's mistress because of their anger and humiliation. This is not wise because it brings the wife to the level of the mistress. In any case, there is no guarantee that the husband will stop seeing that woman or the woman will leave him alone.

I recall many years ago, a wife who told me that she went to the mistress's home, and demanded the return of a gift from her husband. Believe it; this is true! Wives who became extremely angry upon the discovery of infidelity have taken their revenge on a mistress. On the reverse, there are mistresses who have abused wives, both verbally and physically. *There are no winners in infidelity.*

In some situations, the wife might respond with passivity and this will do one of two things. First, the husband may use this behaviour as an indication to go ahead and do what he enjoys. So he continues without remorse or shame. Second, he may perceive his wife's passivity as a way of communicating to him that she does not love him and no longer cares. So, he continues with his adultery.

In either of these two situations, the wife might be so overwhelmed with her shame that she struggles with the embarrassment and is not even aware of her attitudes.

In addition, other factors will create internal problems for the injured wife that will affect the communication pattern in the relationship. She might also use defense mechanisms of avoidance or denial making her behaviour appears to be compliant. In such a setting, the husband does not understand his wife's response towards his infidelity; while the wife is facing intra-psychic struggles in an attempt to understand what is happening to the marriage.

The husband too, might eventually begin experiencing guilt so that he cannot look his wife in the face. That guilt might ignite arguments that will set the stage for interpersonal conflicts to occur. Ultimately, the partners will display their disagreements in quarrels, distancing, and frequent angry outbursts. While there are many fleeting thoughts coming in and out of her mind, the wife might ask herself questions concerning her sexuality and attractiveness.

For *Erica*, she compared herself with her husband's 'friend' stating that the friend was younger. [*In nearly every case, the interloper is younger*]. This is typical of men!

Another woman might wonder, "Where is God?" and "Why has He abandoned me?"

Faith blamed herself for the infidelity and her husband's rejection. Those struggles will create severe emotional problems in the relationship that will affect everyone, including the children.

Nevertheless, the management of interpersonal conflict after infidelity must be in a non-violent environment with professionals who can be objective and sincere. It makes no sense for the couple who are spewing blazing fire against each other with angry words and innuendoes to resolve the situation by themselves. When this happens, each one would be in a subjective mood in an attempt to win the fight. Instead, it would be a win/lose, or lose/lose outcome.

Chapter 41

The Biblical Perspectives on Marital Problems

The Bible does not encourage separation or divorce when problems arise in the relationship.[59] What it teaches is that the couple should seek for reconciliation even if they had to separate for a time. God knows that while we live here on earth, we will always face insurmountable situations that will test us to the height of endurance. All kinds of problems and situations often annoy and make us irritable and uncomfortable.

In the institution of marriage, similar to all other relationships, there will be times of distress and painful experiences. When they occur, this may cause a crushing blow to the self-esteem, dreams and desires. However, in many cases the couple is able to weather those storms with prayer, faith, trust, and confidence in God.

Despite those inevitable vicissitudes to the marital experience, the Bible specifically points to some major principles for marital problem solving. For example, although infidelity is sin and hurtful, it can be understood that anger is associated with its exposure. The emotion of anger can become intense and very destructive because of the shock upon the discovery of a husband's dishonesty.

Nevertheless, the Christian wife must not let anger rule her life. Although she gets angry over the display of disrespect towards her, the Bible teaches to *"Be angry and sin not: let not the sun go down upon your wrath"* (Ephesians 4:26).

Therefore, if the injured wife gives way to the emotion of anger, that person is giving the enemy a foothold into the already fractured

---

[59] I Corinthians 7

relationship. Eventually, this will lead to other destructive behaviours that will create interpersonal conflicts.

With *Rita,* she was so enraged when she heard of her husband's unfaithfulness that she began screaming and hitting him as he was entering the door.

Sally directed her anger inside and did not fight, not because she accepted the behaviour, but because she was just too angry to speak. As a result, she bore hatred for her husband for many years while they still shared the family home.

Alice said, "I heard about his adulteries, and on top of that he was physically abusing me. I sat on my bed and cried because I was so angry, that I wanted to kill him. This was only a momentary thought, and I quickly got over it."

Managing Anger

Being angry is not sinful. However, there are two perspectives relating to the emotion of anger. First, *"feeling angry,"* is easily diffused, because it is the primary stage when there is an analysis of the issues. At this initial stage, emotions are controlled and behaviours modified, while the heightened feelings subside to de-escalate conflict. What happens is that the individual thinks about the consequences of inappropriate actions. The wife will consider the impact of her behaviour on the children and her self-respect; therefore she deals with her emotions in a constructive manner.

The second stage, *"being angry,"* occurs when there is no analysis for anger, and actions and words precede rational thinking. The individual acts on impulse as a defense mechanism, which is harmful and usually escalates into destructive conflict.

In such a situation, there is an intense desire for the injured wife to get even with her husband. It is a time of emotional stimulation when adrenalin seeps into the system to feed the ego, and motivates the emotions of humiliation and anxiety to do something about the hurt. It is really a chain reaction in response to the feelings of hurt pride, overwhelming shame, and deep disappointment.

Nonetheless, if anger resides in a person's heart, it leads to bitterness. Ephesians 4:27, 31-32, reads: *"Let all bitterness, and wrath, and anger,...be put away from you, with all malice...forgiving one another, even as God for Christ's sake has forgiven you."*

Consequently, by forgiving a wrong, the injured spouse is acting in obedience to God, while simultaneously alleviating the presence of interpersonal conflicts and emotional pain. This action does not mean overlooking the wrong, but a demonstration of patience and trust in God to lead and direct in the right path.

It is important to note that we cannot fight spiritual warfare with carnal weapons[60] of anger, hatred, malice, and resentment. If an aggrieved wife employed those methods, then the enemy will have a field day for the complete destruction of the relationship. Additionally, problem-solving in marital conflicts does not mean the injured wife will not be angry after the exposure of infidelity.

What it means is that she will assess her feelings towards her husband, the effect of the adultery on her and her family, the consequences of her actions to decide how she will face the situation.

Taking this route might not happen spontaneously, but as the woman considers the circumstances and consequences, she will act in a manner that will satisfy her mind. Additionally, her motives will depend on her relationship with the Lord, her self-esteem, her children, and the goals she has for the future.

Furthermore, as the wife thinks about what *really* makes her angry; she might plan how to prayerfully, confidently and constructively, deal with feelings of embarrassment, frustration, hurt, and rejection. This proactive approach will place her into a better position, and ultimately prevent the destructive side of anger. It is essential at this stage for the

---

[60] II Corinthians 10

injured wife to recognize that God has not rejected her. Therefore, her anger can be controlled in a constructive and productive manner. After anger, the feeling of rejection seems to be the next emotion that appears.

Clarice:

> *Although I felt hurt and angry when I found out that my husband had been cheating on me, I was willing to take him back. It was hard at first, but when he continued with his behaviour after our second child was born, I felt total rejection. I felt that I was not important to him anymore. I still waited for him with the hope that he would have returned to me. I was devastated because I never thought that he would have left me again. I tried to keep calm and spent time with my children, even though my heart was breaking from the disappointment.*

Incidentally, when a mother displays the right responses before her children, she will be modeling good conflict management skills that will help them to deal with their own problems.

Another way in which she can deal with problems is to seek for outside help. Most of all, she must allow the Holy Spirit to teach and instruct her about what actions to take to restore harmony into *her* life, even if not into the marriage (Psalm 32:8). In any case, there must be a time for healing, and the process for grief to take place after the exposure of infidelity.

Conflicts will develop in any relationship, and marital situations seem to be the most prominent target since the individuals are so closely connected. Still, it would be unwise to treat problems as though they do not exist because this would be living in denial and fantasy.

Finally, it is just as disastrous to cover up or keep anger inside as when it is explosive. Therefore, it is better to deal with the emotion rather than smother it.

Dealing with Problems

Begin and end with prayer. Next, the *first* step is by acknowledging the existence of problems and owning up to personal faults. It is better to recognize and accept the reality that there are problems, especially when the children ask questions. Hiding the truth from them is not using good judgment. Instead, the facts should be explained in a manner that is equivalent to their age and emotional health.

Second, the partners should have open, but private discussions to identify issues of hurts and embarrassment and talk with each other about those situations.[61] For example, if the problem is lack of finance or overspending, then deal with those issues and do not pretend. The couple should not lie to each other or hide feelings and the pain that is being felt. Instead, they should be honest about expressing those feelings without fear or intimidation. Additionally, it would help greatly to include the Holy Spirit in all discussions, and the use of pertinent Scriptures as guide.

Third, each individual should face the issues by identifying and admitting to personal faults. The Bible teaches that we should *"confess our faults,"*[62] and this can only be done when there is honesty in expressing feelings. In addition, each person should take time to listen when the other is talking.

Finally, there must be mutual decisions on how the problems will be resolved, either together or with outside help. However, it does not make sense to delay in seeking for help if there is hope in restoring the relationship to an amicable resolution.

Further, it is important that whatever each person says during the time of problem solving, it will not be under the influence of emotional outbursts. For this reason, it is vital that issues are clearly identified, and separated from personalities. The partners should not verbally assault each other in an attempt to win an argument, nor should they talk over each other. This is not the character of a Christian.

---

[61] Matthew 18:15
[62] James 5:16

Chapter 42

Some Reasons for Marital Conflict

Marital conflict occurs when partners speak impulsively without thinking of the consequences because someone has lost respect for the other. They hurt each other with name-calling and blame. Sometimes there is the use of hurtful insults, put-downs, and even physical abuse. Either of the individuals might make wild threats in a taunting manner to see how the other one will react. Depending on the response, the conflict situation will blow over or explode into outright *war*. In some cases, the abuses get stronger and more frequent, and the distancing begins with a combination of malice, silence, and other destructive behaviours.

The reasons for marital conflicts include the following:

Defensiveness

Couples who are stuck in a defensive mode will use criticisms and insults against each other. They can also become critical and judgmental with the least infraction, and those behaviours will delay or prevent a successful resolution.[63] Moreover, holding on to hidden agendas and imposing one's values on another would prevent the successful outcome of interpersonal conflicts.[64]

Manipulations

Many times conflicts arise because one person demands that the other upholds religious principles, maybe because it is what a religion requires. There are religious organizations that insist on the affiliation

---

[63] D. Gouran; W.E. Wiethoff; and J.A. Doelger, *Mastering Communication*. 2nd. ed. (Boston: Allyn and Bacon, 1994).

[64] Ibid

of the entire family. In some cases, one partner became a Christian after the fact. In any event the couple should use wisdom and knowledge in proceeding to a mutually agreeable understanding when it comes to religion.

Even if the wife became a Christian after marriage, she should understand that her husband has the right to decide whether he wants to follow her or not. It is not her duty to force him to attend church with the use of threats or by withholding sex from him.

The wife should continue with her duties and treat her husband with respect and love. It would help greatly if she informs her husband of the types of social activities she will participate in, rather than suddenly change things over night. *He is still the leader in the home.*

Control

Another reason for manipulation is the husband who believes he must *control* his wife with any warped and immoral behaviours. Manipulation is a form of witchcraft from which domestic violence is spawned. For example, take *Zoë*. She was married to *Burt*. He was an ordinary go to work, to church, and home person.

However, *Zoë* was an achiever and wanted to continue with her education. *Burt* opposed to her desire and insisted that he did not marry a "student," he married a wife. This developed into arguments that eventually led to the dissolution of the marriage.

Another husband wanted his wife home all of the time. He would say to her, "You give up that job or else…I want you here when I get home." Those behaviours present a state of manipulation and control. Any woman, living under those conditions is demeaning herself, because she has no courage either to seek for help, or to end the relationship.

Emotional Abuse

Moreover, the wife who lives with a husband who treats her as his property will live in constant fear, low self-esteem, and lack of self-confidence. She lives in compliance under the dominance of her husband who is being possessive. That type of behaviour represents an example of emotional abuse.

Husbands like those, usually take the Scriptures out of context, by quoting Bible verses to make the wife feels guilty. One of those popular verses in paraphrase is, "You are to be subject to me. That is what the Bible says." Any wife who lacks self-worth will fall into the clutches of such an oppressor, who will squeeze out every drop of self-confidence making her senseless to his abuses. There are other forms of abuses that will create the environment for marital conflicts resulting in all kinds of domestic abuses.

Insensitivity

In the case of marriage, the individuals are in "close physical proximity to each other where there are many sensory channels used, and feedback is immediate."[65] This is so true because with the wife who is used to getting a hug or kiss when her husband leaves and this suddenly stops, it will create suspicions. His expressions of love were evidence of his way of communicating to her that, "Honey, I love you and no other."

The husband too, will become conscious when his wife does not respond to him in a loving way. Each one must be sensitive to the feelings of the other. This sensitivity works both ways. Furthermore, those expressions of tenderness and love are communication signals requiring reciprocity; otherwise, someone will be disappointed.

Effective communication is an exchange from a sender to a receiver who responds to the signal. However, if one partner sends out a signal that drops like lead in the sea and there is no inter-change this gives cause for emotional response that can motivate interpersonal conflict.

Disrespect of each other

The writers further added that with relation to interpersonal communication, we have many different types of relationships with

---

[65] Ibid

"people view each other as unique individuals, and not as people who are simply acting out social situations."[66] Obviously, it is important that couples recognize these factors to avoid the destructive side of interpersonal conflicts in the marital relationship. They must each acknowledge, appreciate, and respect their individualities, and the differences in their roles and personalities.

The main point is having effective conflict management skills and knowing how to use them to de-escalate interpersonal conflict when it occurs.

What is most important is that since they will have relationships with different people for whom they often make allowances, they should also keep the integrity of their own relationship intact. They should not ignore the fact that since they respect others, they should also respect each other.

Quid Pro Quo

This is the "give and take" attitude, whereby one partner will only do something if he or she is compensated in return. Those attitudes are dangerous, because they distract attention from problems, thus preventing discussion in order to find solutions for resolution.

Uncontrolled Emotions

A further reason why conflicts will occur in the marital relationship is the fact that emotions influence conflict situations. There are times when anger overcomes an individual, and this can be volatile and cause hurt to the other person. It does not matter that there was no physical attack. One of those times could be one spouse choosing words that are hurtful to the other.

Before speaking, each one should take into consideration *how* the response will affect the recipient; *what* the consequences might be; the *place* of the event; and *who* is present, to determine if a delayed

---

[66] Ibid

response would be better. To delay the response does not mean avoidance, but it will be a decision that will often de-escalate conflict.

Unquestionably, conflicts will always be present in all interpersonal relationships depending on the way people communicate with one another, and how they respond to crises. Furthermore, because there are few participants involved, interpersonal communication differs from other forms of communication.

Other factors that will inhibit successful interpersonal conflict include "indifference, lack of commitment and openness, poor communication skills, negative body language, individual perceptions, and dominance."[67]

Undoubtedly, any or a combination of factors may prolong marital conflict causing greater problems to occur in the relationship. Besides, partners are not always aware of their own attitudes that contribute to the breakdown of the marriage.

The biblical perspective for the effective management of marital is vital for an amicable and peaceful resolution and the life of the marriage. Therefore, partners must deal with problems in a timely way and move away from past injustices by choosing to forgive one another.

---

[67] Ibid

Chapter 43

Reactions to Problems

Researchers have identified several problems that typically arise in interpersonal conflict situations.[68] To begin with, at the initial stage of any conflict, the disputants may display pretense concerning the status of the relationship.

For example, in the case of a wife, she might tell herself and others that "no such thing as cheating has happened," and that "it is only malicious gossip" about her husband. Some will even compromise the behaviour in an attempt to deal with it. Using those tactics will compound the situation and further destroy the relationship between the couple. The result will be in the demonstration disrespect and low self-confidence.

Theorists on interpersonal conflict agree that this behaviour can be damaging and may lead to future problems. Hardly does anyone need empirical research to understand that to take this avenue is venturing into the enemy's path of deceit, confusion, and destruction.

In addition, in a marital dispute situation, very rarely would any of the parties assume blame for the breakdown of the relationship. At least one of them or both will sometimes avoid talking about problems. Instead, each one will blame the other with various reasons for the marital dispute.

Blaming the other person can be destructive because one partner may begin to assassinate the other's character or even family members as the cause for the presenting problem.

---

[68] D. Gouran; W.E. Wiethoff; and J.A. Doelger, *Mastering Communication.* 2nd. ed. (Boston: Allyn and Bacon, 1994).

Referring to the problems of denial and avoidance, it could well be that if the issues were dealt with earlier there might not have been a breakdown in the relationship. In addition, if they pretend that no problems exist, this can be a sign of repression or denial. Both are unhealthy and destructive to the individuals and to the relationship.

Nevertheless, the most destructive type of reaction to marital interpersonal conflict is the "empty relationship," where "partners speak in an exaggeratedly affectionate way, but deliberately act in ways that show contempt, disdain, or irritation."[69]

Those types of behaviours are destructive to their relationship because they only create a stifled environment. When those behaviours are present in the marriage they can lead to emotional abuse because, the truth is that the wife is no longer interested in having intimate relations with her husband. It is all a façade and behind closed doors, or in certain social settings the situation changes.

Furthermore, when couples bury the existence of problems, they are adopting the "ostrich" style of behaviour, and this will escalate interpersonal problems in the marriage

If a wife finds herself in such a situation, she will suffer various types of emotional problems that can lead to low self-esteem, and even depression.

---

[69] S. Duck, (cited Hagestad and Smyer, 1982), *Understanding Relationships*. (The Guildford Press, 1991).

Chapter 44

Resolving Marital Conflicts

If the parties reach an agreement concerning the issues in the relationship, it is then time to deal with each one in a safe non-threatening environment. They must move away from past hurts and honestly deal with the issues with forgiveness in order to move on with their lives, whether together or individually.

Nevertheless, writers are of the opinion that if the couple focuses on each other's goals and desires, this approach will help to avoid using a win/lose strategy. Marital conflict can be resolved amicably in various constructive ways, such as the following:

Concentrate

This means that each partner gives equal attention to the feelings of the other in order to eliminate both the need to be defensive and the need to escape when conflicts arise. This focus of attention will help both of them to show empathy and compassion for each other.

For example, a statement such as, *"I can understand why you might think that way,"* will help to convince the other partner that it is all right to feel whatever emotion is going on, even in the midst of a highly charged conflict situation.

Being passive and accepting in a discussion will not resolve problems. However, by paying attention during the resolution process, one person will recognize hurts and pain the other one is experiencing. These might have gone unnoticed for a long time, but is now in the open. The revelation will be an opportunity to do something about any problems that become evident during this time.

Being Present

In this context, by paying attention each partner is not just hearing words, but is thinking seriously on what the other is saying. It is most important that they each attempt to understand what the other is saying, rather than seeking for personal attention. This is a positive attitude towards resolution because it gives a specific sense of relief to the speaker knowing that the other person is focussing, and is present. This act of awareness on what a partner is saying and feeling will minimize the need to defend actions, and thereby de-escalate conflict. Furthermore, there is a keen sense of feeling secure in a non-threatening safe environment for discussion that is free from fear of recriminations.

Respect

If the parties are in a non-threatening safe environment, they can handle interpersonal conflicts in a respectful, sincere, and honest manner. Thoughts will not be on hurting each other with destructive descriptive scripts to humiliate and embarrass the other person. There will be no temptation for physical hurts or emotional outbursts. Besides, each partner will give the other an equal chance to speak and to share feelings. In a setting where a third party is present, it is very important that the mediator gives each individual the same opportunity to speak.

Exposure

When the couple feels the sense of trust and honesty, there will be no reason to be embarrassed when revealing hidden secrets or feelings held from each other, maybe for a long time. Sometimes it is fear of expressing oneself that results in emotional outbursts and anger because the individual is stifling real feelings. When the couple brings those feelings out into the open there will be a deeper sense of commitment, loyalty and love towards each other. The revelation enables them to feel and understand each other's hurts with empathy and compassion, instead of concentrating on what the other partner did to cause hurt.

Moreover, the free exchange of ideas and personal desires are fundamental factors to take into consideration for the management and resolution of marital interpersonal conflicts. For example, if there is conscious effort to encourage open dialogue, with the interchange of views and opinions, this will support both parties in a marital dispute, and enhance the communication process.

Expressing Emotions

One of the attributes of emotions is that they are communicable. Therefore, when one partner sees the other as a wounded person in need of healing, interest will transfer from that person's pain to the other, in order to bring peace and comfort. For instance, if the husband is remorseful and shows signs of this, the injured wife might have second thoughts about divorce. This will alter the whole setting from conflict to resolution and reconciliation. The presence and recognition of interpersonal conflicts in any marriage need not be a bad thing for the couple. Instead, it can be a time of reflective listening, understanding, and exposure of problems in the relationship.

Third Party Intervention

The partners must be confident that they will equally benefit from the outcome of the discussions, whatever the resolution might be. For this reason, it would be wise to seek outside intervention where a third party will view the situation from an objective perspective. However, if there is confidence, there must also be trust that revelations made in the discussions are true. This means that each individual will own up to personal faults. In addition, there must be mutual agreement that the couple will accept the final decisions. Nevertheless, resolution cannot be made without faith, understanding, confidence, trust, love, and respect for each other.

Reconciliation

The Bible teaches that Christians have a ministry of reconciliation, given to them by God. It is therefore imperative to use this ministry to mend broken marital relationships. In any case, reconciliation cannot take place until the individuals identify problems, and are willing to accept the process and terms for resolution.

What is reconciliation? It means that the couple will agree to let go of past hurts, insults, and bad behaviours. They must be willing to settle their differences without any desire to keep records of each other's faults. However, until they each reveal the things that are bothering them, nothing will work. Holding back grudges and resentment for future mistakes will only make matters worse for both of them. Therefore, trust, openness, honesty, sincerity, and loyalty are vital for resolving and maintaining the relationship.

Another valid point is that unless there is a determined effort towards sincere forgiveness, there can be no reconciliation. Furthermore, the process for reconciliation will not be complete without the presence of forgiveness because it is the final step in resolving interpersonal conflicts.

Obviously, there are spiritual, psychological, and emotional losses pertaining to infidelity. Therefore, during the discussion, the couple should communicate any feelings of guilt or remorse in order to complete the reconciliation process.

To conclude this chapter, the couple must deal with interpersonal problems before they lead to disastrous situations resulting in one partner straying from the marital union.

Moreover, when there is a break in the relationship, it would not be advisable for either partner to take a conservative attitude to ignore the problem. God's plan has always been for unity and love in the home. Moreover, the Bible strongly emphasized, *"Husbands, love your wives, and be not bitter against them"* (Colossians 3:19).

Whatever the reasons for conflicts, they must not be ignored. There must be honesty in acknowledging issues and dealing with them in a timely manner. This will lead to discussions from both the positive and negative perspectives, which is vital to the health of the marital relationship. Furthermore, the way the couple resolve interpersonal conflicts is important, since the family is the most important social system whereby children learn, and emulate behaviours from parents.

Marital interpersonal conflict can be just as destructive as any other conflicts if it is not de-escalated. Therefore, it must be controlled and handled in a non-threatening atmosphere where each person can discuss and listen to the reasons for the disagreement that caused the problems in the relationship. The consensus among writers is that interpersonal conflict is inevitable in all human relationships.

Finally, the way the disputants handle interpersonal conflicts with a mediator will affect the outcome of the discussions. Therefore, it is very important that each individual *knows* what he/she wants to accomplish out of the discussion with honesty and sincerity.

Besides, in order to have an agreeable result, they *must* employ the right strategies with effective problem-solving skills to restore balance to the relationship.

Chapter 45

Forgiveness and Infidelity

The Bible teaches that before God will accept our gifts, we must first be reconciled with an offender.[70] Therefore, unless the couple is willing to be open and vulnerable with truthfulness, forgiveness cannot take place. It is easy to say, "I forgive you" even when it is not from the heart. Nevertheless, to reach the goal, the partners must each take the first step, and that is confession and admission of faults.

If everyone recognizes that we are all sinful beings with the old adamic nature in us, there will be sensitivity on the part of both the adulterer and the injured party. Forgiveness can soften the blow of infidelity, especially when the offender is remorseful and shows evidence that the behaviour will not be repeated.

In addition, forgiveness can help to heal hurts and resolve problems that will occur between partners, and this will keep the bond of marriage intact. It is true that there is hurt and humiliation from infidelity, but a forgiving spirit coupled with love can alleviate those pains and brighten the dark shades of distressful feelings for the injured.

Essentially, forgiveness between partners is important because an unforgiving spirit robs the partners of the ingredients of peace, joy, trust, and harmony that are necessary in a marital relationship.

Forgiveness is not an Elixir

Nevertheless, forgiveness is not an elixir, but when exercised by the injured to an offender it helps to heal wounds and to restrain the work

---

[70] Matthew 5:23-25

of the enemy. It also relieves the injured wife from holding on to grudges and resentment that will keep her in bondage. Moreover, an unforgiving partner leaves the door open, giving the enemy an advantage to create havoc with the relationship between herself and God (*See* Ephesians 4:27).

For example, in a case where there is proof of infidelity, there must be forgiveness. Otherwise, God will not forgive the unforgiving person (*See* Matthew 6:14-15). Furthermore, if the injured wife holds on to grudges, she may be hurting only herself and no one else.

Additionally, an unforgiving spirit causes bitterness to take root in the heart of the unforgiving spouse resulting in blame, hostility, and the holding of malice and hard feelings. Those attitudes will place the individual in mental and spiritual bondage as is seen in the case of the unforgiving servant in the passage (*See* Matthew 18:18-35).

The act of forgiveness does not mean excusing or overlooking infidelity. No one can deny the fact that the woman was violated by the act of her husband's behaviour. Nevertheless in order to regain her self respect, peace of mind, and relationship with the Lord she must forgive.[71]

Forgiveness further means that the injured is willing to work with her husband with the hope of ending the adulterous behaviour. Moreover, both the wife and the husband need to forgive each other, especially where there have been open insults and verbal attacks.

Infidelity is harsh and cruel, but the injured can overcome the inclination to retaliate or seek revenge. In many instances, if partners would think through the problems in the marriage, and find out how they can deal with those issues before the situation gets out of hand, there might be many more marriages saved. Taking time to analyze the problems carefully will lead to forgiveness; and acknowledging faults will result in compassion for each other.

---

[71] Matthew 6:14-15

Still, let us not think that forgiveness is an easy act to perform. It is hard to forgive, especially in the case of adultery. Therefore, the injured must take time to think through the situation, and go through the process the best way she can.

The Dual Work of Forgiveness

The dual work forgiveness takes place in the heart of the injured. In the first place, it will begin to heal the wounds that caused the suffering, so that the person can see things clearly and think wisely. Secondly, forgiveness will lift the burden of hurt and help the person go through the grieving period with less anger and frustration.

Moreover, the gift of forgiveness will be in complete obedience to God's Word and His plan for dealing with problems. When the injured wife renders forgiveness to her adulterous husband, this is an expression of a submissive attitude, respect, and love towards God.

Despite, the effect and work of sincere forgiveness, we cannot rest on any false assumptions that it will act as a deterrent to stop the offender from repeating the behaviour. This decision comes from the heart after the perpetrator has confessed, asked God's forgiveness, and truly repented.

The Process of Forgiveness

1. ***Enlisting the Holy Spirit:*** The Bible states *"Likewise the Spirit helpeth our infirmities: for we know not what we ought to pray for as we ought..."* (Romans 8:26a). We need the Holy Spirit to direct us in our prayers. The reason is that we cannot pray effectively for someone who has wounded us unless we ask the Holy Spirit to help us. This is even more so, in the situation of adultery because the hurt is still very fresh. Moreover, all the negative emotions are evident. Therefore, the injured must ask for guidance and direction to know how to pray for her husband. Eventually, the wife who enlists the Holy Spirit's presence will see her husband as a sick soul who needs healing.

2.   *Effective Prayer:* Since may be in a better spiritual position than her husband, she should demonstrate this by praying for him. I am not saying that the husband will return; there is no guarantee about that. However, after she has done her part, she can ask the Holy Spirit to help her see the husband through the eyes of Jesus. Similar to wearing a pair of spectacles for better vision when our eyes need them, so it is when we pray for an offender. From our mortal perspectives, we can only see the wrong done to us. This blur will block out the vision of Jesus. Similarly, for our prayers to be effective we must see an offender as Jesus would; wounded, and deceived by Satan's lies, and also as a result of his own disobedience to God's Word. When Jesus was on the Cross he uttered these words, *"Father, forgive them; for they know not what they do"* (Luke 23:34). This prayer was an earnest plea for sinful man. He was not looking at our sins and wickedness; no, he saw sin sick souls that only *his* Blood could change. In light of that, he was willing to die for us.

3.   *Pray for love for the adulterer*: Did I say love? Yes, I did. It is almost impossible to forgive without love. This is a special kind of love; and not one, which is romantic. When the offender prays for love for the adulterer, that person will feel relief from anger, resentment, and the temptation to be vindictive or to retaliate.

4.   *Pray for the adulterer:* In Matthew 5:44 Jesus said, *"Love your enemies, bless them that curse you, do good to them that hate you, and pray for them which despitefully use you, and persecute you"* (*See* also Luke 6:27, 28).

Obviously, the basis for the process of forgiveness is sincere prayer for the adulterer. If the injured wife follows these four suggestions, she can live a life free from animosity and hostility towards her husband. This does not mean that change will come overnight, nor does it mean that the marriage might not end in divorce. What this does, is free the injured wife of the weight of negative emotions that will keep her bowed beneath the load of malice, resentment, and hostilities.

Clearly, the process for reconciliation cannot be complete unless both parties in the situation forgive each other. Agreeably, forgiveness is a process, and it may not happen immediately, but it only takes the first step and the others will follow. It will be not easy because there is the desire to seek vindication in any way possible. Nevertheless, when the injured goes before God, she should say *exactly* how she feels, even between sobs, "tell it like it is."[72]

I am angry! I am hurting all over! God, I hate him!
Why did You let this happen to me?
How could You not have prevented this from happening to me?
I am a good wife, Christian, mother.
I do not deserve this treatment, and so forth.

Listen, He will not be surprised, and you will feel a lot better when you get off your knees. God wants honesty when we come before Him. Additionally, follow the instructions found in Philippians 4:6-7. After you have purged out your bad feelings, you will notice that the pain begins to subside. You will be a lighter, fresher person ready to make whatever decisions you need to make. If you are angry, *do not make any decisions*, because you might later regret them.

---

[72] Philippians 4:6-7

Think about the following questions

1. Do I still love my husband?
2. Am I willing to forgive my husband?
3. Is my husband a good provider?
4. Should I talk things over with my husband?
5. Does he want to talk with me?
6. Should I tell our children?
7. How do I feel about the marriage/my husband/myself/God?
8. Is it better to divorce my husband?
9. Do I want to save the marriage?
10. Can I trust my husband again?
11. What contribution did I make to the breakdown of the marriage?
12. How committed am I to this relationship?
13. Is my husband the *only* one at fault?
14. How dutiful was I/he to the marriage relationship?
15. This is the last time I will ever trust him/another man again.
16. What can I do to re-build this marriage?
17. Do I really care about my husband?
18. How can I change the situation?
19. What am I willing to do/give/change to improve this marriage?
20. Should we both get outside help?
21. What does this relationship means to me?
22. Should I help my husband break up this family?
23. Do I want to speak to him again?
24. Is there hope for us/the marriage?

Although forgiveness is an act of fulfilling God's will, the injured wife cannot do so without His grace and the Holy Spirit. Moreover, the whole root of forgiveness hangs on love.

The Bible sums it up this way, *"If a man say, I love God, and hateth his brother, he is a liar: for he that loveth not his brother whom he hath seen, how can he love God whom he hath not seen?"* (I John 4:20. *See* also John 3:16; I John 1:6-10; 2:9-11).

209

Part VII
Reflections from the Research
Case Studies of Wives Living With Their Unfaithful Husbands

This section may only be of interest to those who are pursuing a study in women's affairs, and want to gain insight into the activities of the research.

The section covers:
- Reflections on the Research
- Glossary
- References
- Index
- Appendices
  - Research Questions
  - Letter to Informants
  - Consent Form

Chapter 46
Reflections from the Research

Case Studies of Wives Living With Their Unfaithful Husbands

Research Approach and Type

The aim of the research was to find out why women stayed with their unfaithful husbands, and the relationship of infidelity and interpersonal conflict.

For the exercise, I used the qualitative research approach method to answer the research question [*See* Appendix I]. From the major question, there were four other subsidiary questions.

In order for me to have obtained *reliability* and *validity* of the research, the scripts from the participants enabled me to triangulate the raw data with the informal conversations, and the literature reviewed in the study.

The main strength of *qualitative research* is that it can identify issues of concern to specific population, seen in the emergent categories and themes from this research [*See* Appendix II].

The study further revealed similarities among the participants, with thematic patterns of negative behaviours upon the discovery of infidelity.

It is important for the reader to understand, that the results of this study is not comprehensive for all women who remain with their unfaithful husbands.

Moreover, the sample selected for the study was on purpose; therefore, the outcome cannot be a representation for all women who remain in an unfaithful situation.

During the interviews, the women reported that they felt humiliation, frustration, and embarrassment upon their discovery of infidelity.

However, anger appeared to be the most prominent emotional response that influenced the impact of the discovery of the behaviour.

For many of the women, they displayed their anger openly. Whereas for others, the anger was covert, and the response to the discovery was silence, because they feared the impact and outcome of the result in themselves or to their husbands.

Apparently, interpersonal conflict has emerged to be a major factor from the result of infidelity.

Since marriage is an adventure for newly married couples, it is imperative that each party makes proper preparation for the eventualities that will develop as is found in all adventures in life. This does not mean that one can effectively predict what will happen. Nevertheless, some situations could be prevented if the parties had made proper preparations. I would infer that most people would admit that if they had known certain things beforehand, then they would have made different choices in marriage.

Outcome of Findings
The findings agreed with the literature, revealing that in some relationships, there is denial to the existence of interpersonal conflict, and this presents a greater challenge for any couple in a marital setting.

The implication is that, when interpersonal conflicts are hidden, the next step would be to find some type of immediate escape to fill the gap, especially when partners are not communicating with each other.

The study showed that in many instances, the wife did not make her feelings known to her husband. Still, in some situations, the revelation did not change the behaviour.

Consequently, if couples do not confront each other, admit when there are problems in the marriage, and deal with them in a constructive manner, then they are heading for disaster. One can only imagine that in many of the situations that led to infidelity and divorce, if the partners were honest and open with facing their problems, this destructive social catalyst might not have ventured into their path.

Additionally, the study showed that infidelity is a devastating social disease that creates havoc in the lives of married people. An informant described it as, "a constant sword in my bosom."

However, this seems to be a paradoxical situation, because although this woman felt this way, (she was not the only one) yet she remained in the marriage for many decades, despite the dissatisfaction and unhappiness. She explained that she stayed because of her commitment to the marriage and her relationship with the Lord.

Further, the findings are in agreement with the literature, reporting that emotional responses follow the knowledge of infidelity (Buunk & Bakker, 1997), which suggests the inevitable presence of an emotion such as anger.

All the women reported various types of emotions that they felt, with anger being the most prevalent upon the discovery of their husbands' infidelity.

Evidently, emotions play a significant role in the response to infidelity whether the injured person is saint or sinner. Those feelings will not always result in destructive behaviours because the injured wife can emotionally attach herself to, and become concerned with the welfare of her husband.

For some wives this leads to a motivation to continue with the relationship despite the dissatisfaction.

Buunk & Bakker further noted that research shows that high commitment promotes a high willingness to accommodate. The responses from the interview questions support this point because most of the women were willing to accept the situation. In some cases they revealed an attitude of, "I cannot do anything about his behaviour." It may seem nonsensical to the reader for women to remain with their unfaithful husbands, but the women may have their own personal reasons for remaining.

The women in this study all shared similarities of rage, feelings of betrayal, shock, tension, anxiety, depression, hurt, emotional pain, and confusion, which are evidences of interpersonal and intra-psychic conflicts.

These were evident from the reports of withdrawal, need for physical attack, and silence to their husbands, and escaping when he returns after his long absence.

The research findings further revealed that the women were unanimous in emphasizing that marriage is a permanent sacred covenant ordained by God, no matter how they felt about the consequences of their husbands' infidelity.

They believed that by leaving their husbands, divorcing him or treating him badly would be a violation of their faith and walk with God. Therefore, they endured the behaviour even though it caused pain and humiliation.

Literature and Data
The literature and raw data were synonymous in stating that both children and women suffer from the result of infidelity. I noticed that the women expressed deep sensitivity and over-protectiveness towards their children.

Obviously, the women in the study have shown extreme courage for the interview, and to tell their stories with such details. It was their secrets, their experiences, and their lives; yet they trusted me to intrude upon such personal and painful histories. I also believe that they represent a class of women who portray extreme strength, courage, and faith in God.

Expectedly, many of the women still have a trace of hostility against their husbands. However, a few of them are working through the anger and frustration by getting professional help and re-affirming their relationship with God.

My encounter with the women was a great opportunity for many, because it was the first time they had ever ventured to tell anyone about their marital problems in details. One woman told me that she felt "so much better" since talking with me.

213

I discovered then, that infidelity was not a subject that attracts discussion even in private among friends because of fear of being seen as "foolish" when a woman remains with her unfaithful husband.

Moreover, I further discovered that mention of the behaviour is rare, unless it was in informal conversations, and only as an aside.

This research revealed to me that women could become extremely strong and determined, despite the devastating effects of infidelity. This is one point not mentioned in the literature reviewed for this study.

When I asked the women how they coped with living with their husbands, the report showed that many of them spent much time crying, with sleepless and lonely nights. Others prayed, went to church, and just got more involved with the bringing up and nurturing of their children.

However, they were all very protective towards the children, and in many cases, kept quarrels with their husbands away from them. There were also those women who continued with their lives by improving themselves. One particular woman went back to school in order to obtain a better job.

Many of the women remained because they had made financial and other investments of time and labour that they were not willing to release to another woman. Therefore, they found inner resources or external activities to ease the pain and frustrations.

In terms of the management of interpersonal, conflict, one woman reported, "I have learned to be calm so that I no longer say anything to my husband." She said this with resignation in her voice and attitude.

Others quarreled, or ignored the husband. In some situation, the woman ordered the husband out of the bedroom, or she would move to another room. These responses are common in most dysfunctional marital relationships.

Disappointingly, as mentioned before, many churches do not have resources for helping members who have suffered from the infidelities of their husbands.

Really, some pastors seem to be of the opinion that professional counseling is humanistic, and therefore it has no place in the church.

My Interpretation of the Findings and Results

Finally, the result of the research revealed that there is a correlation between interpersonal conflict and infidelity.

Additionally, the cognitive inconsistencies from the intra-psychic struggles resulted in an interconnection of spiritual, psychological, emotional, and behavioural problems. The problems became clear as the informants discussed their experiences and the challenges they faced. The sample selected for the research came from a diverse population and spans to more than one region.

This research should be replicated with a larger sample, and with women from all backgrounds, and more widely geographically located.

Glossary of Terms

Born-again Christian: Someone who has received Jesus Christ through water baptism and receiving the Holy Spirit.

Cognitive Dissonance: the non-fitting relations among cognitions. It is also a motivating factor in its own right (Festinger, 1993).

Commitment: A promise or pledge to do something, (American Heritage College Dictionary [AHCD], 1997). (ii) A pledge to marital fidelity for life (Hawkins, 1991).

Communication: The habit of listening, clarifying, summarizing, and paying attention while another person is speaking.

Conflict: A difference in opinion or purpose that frustrates someone's goals or desires (Sande, 1991).

Domestic Abuse: This is any form of abuse, i.e., physical, financial, mental, emotional, sexual, or any behaviour that is inflicted by one partner to the other that will affect the marital relationship.

Infidelity: Sexual intercourse outside of marriage (*See* Exodus 20:14; Matthew 19:9).

Interpersonal Conflict: The emotional interactions between people who are in close proximity with one another.

Intimacy: (i). The physical, emotional, intellectual, sexual, and spiritual aspects of life, that brings wholeness to marriage (Faith for Today, 1991). (ii). Oneness with healthy separateness and the ultimate goal for marriage (Hawkins, (1991).

Intra-Psychic Conflict: Internal confusion with inconsistent thinking.

Marriage Covenant: A covenant before God (Malachi 2:14).

Negative Dissonance: Exists when an individual makes the wrong decisions about a conflicting life event (Vander Zanden, 1998).

Non-verbal Communication: Listening with the use of body language – raised eyebrows, silence, ignoring, etc.

Unequally Yoked: *"Be ye not unequally yoked together with unbelievers: for what fellowship hath righteousness with unrighteousness? And what communion hath light with darkness"* (II Corinthians 6:14). To be unequally yoked in the context of Christianity means, one person is not an active Christian who is following Jesus Christ through water baptism and with the indwelling Holy Spirit. It can also involve other situations such as: religious differences, and so on.

References and Suggested Readings

Anderson, N.T., & C. Mylander. *The Christ Centered Marriage*. Regal Books, 1996.

Brown, E.M. *Patterns of Infidelity and Their Treatment*. Brunner/Mazel Publishers, 1991.

Buchanan, C. *Caught In the Act: A Fascinating Account of Infidelity from All Three Sides*. Thorsons Publishing Group, 1990.

Bunnk, B. "Jealousy as Related to Attributions for the Partner's Behaviour." *Social Psychology Quarterly*, 47, (10), (1984): pp.107-112.

Buunk, B.P., & A.B. Bakker. "Responses to Unprotected Extra-dyadic Sex by One's Partner: Testing Predictions from Interdependence and Equity Theory" *Journal of Research and Sex*, 34, (4), (1997): pp.387-397.

Charny, I.W., & S. Parnass. "The Impact of Extramarital Relationships on the Continuation of Marriages." *Journal of Sex Marital Therapy*, Summer 21, (2), (1995): pp.100-115.

Choi, K.H., J.A. Catania, & M.M. Dolcini, "Extramarital sex and HIV risk behaviour among US adults: results from the National AIDS Behaviour Survey." (*Abstract*). *American Journal of Public Health*, December 1984, 12, (1994): pp. 2003-7.

Colligan, J., & K. "Colligan Forgiveness: The Heart of Love." *The Catholic World*, May-June, 238, 1425, (1995): p.116 (4).

De Gregoris, V. *Christian Understanding of Marriage: The American Baptist Churches. Ecumenical and Pastoral Directives, Massachusetts Commission on Christian Unity*, 1990.

DiBlasio, F.A., & B.B. "Benda Practitioners, Religion and the use of Forgiveness in the Clinical Setting. Special Issue: Religious Values in Psychotherapy." *Journal of Psychology & Christianity*, Summer, 10, (2), (1991): pp. 166-172.

Dolcini, M. et. al. "Demographic Characteristics of Heterosexuals with Multiple Partners: The National AIDS Behaviour Surveys." *Family Planning Perspectives*, 25, (1993): pp.206-214.

Duck, S. *Understanding Relationships*. The Guildford Press, 1991.

_____. *Social and Personal Relationships, in* M. L. Knapp & G.R. Miller (eds.) *Handbook of Interpersonal Communication*, (pp.665-686). Sage, 1985.

Eaker-Weil, B.E., & R. Winter. *Adultery, The Forgivable Sin – Healing the Inherited Patterns of Betrayal in Your Family*. A Birch Lane Press Book Published by Carol Publishing Group, 1993.

Eisenman, T.L. *Temptations Families Face: Braking Patterns That Keep Us Apart*. InterVarsity Press, 1996.

Ekstrom, R.R., *How Media Influences Our Faith and Values: Media, Faith, & Families*. J. Roberto, ed. Don Bosco Multimedia, New Rochelle, NY, 1992.

Elster, J. "Norms of Revenge." *Ethics*, 100 (July 1990): pp.862-885.

Espenshade, T.J. "Marriage Trends in America: Estimates, Implications, and Underlying Causes." *Population and Development Review*, 11, (2), (June 1985), pp.193-241.

Festinger, L. *A Theory of Cognitive Dissonance*. Stanford University, 1963.

Furstenberg, F.F., Jr. "Divorce and the American Family." *Annual Review of Sociology*, 16, (1990): pp. 379-403.

Gerhardt, P. "The Emotional Cost of Infidelity." *Special to the Washington Post*, (Tuesday, March 30 1999): p.10.

Glass, S. "Shattered Vows: Interview with Hara Estroff Marano." *McCall's*, 125, (10), (1998): pp.34-.

Gouran, D., W.E. Wiethoff, & J.A. Doelger. *Mastering Communication.* Second ed. Boston: Allyn and Bacon, 1994.

Hackney, H. & J.M. Bernard. "Dyadic Adjustment Processes in Divorce Counseling." *Journal of Counseling & Development*, 69, (1990): pp.134, 142.

Hawkins, R.E. *Strengthening Marital Intimacy.* Baker Book House, 1991.

Hocker, J.L. & W.W. Wilmot. *Interpersonal Conflict.* Dubuque, 1991.

Hollander, D. "Aspects of Men's Sexual Behaviour Affect Wives' Risk of Cervical Cancer," in Digests. *International Family Planning Perspectives*, 22, (3), (September 1996): p.130.

Jenkins, J., and A.Petersen. *Surround Your Marriage with Hedges*, in *The Christian Family Answer Book*, M. Yorkey, (ed.). Victor Books, 1996.

Klein, C. *How to Forgive When You Can't Forget: Healing Our Relationships.* Berkley Books, 1997.

Knapp, M. *Interpersonal Communication and Human Relationships.* Boston: Allyn and Bacon, 1984.

Kramer, P.D. "Should You Leave? Leaving a Romantic Relationship." *Psychology Today*, 30, (5), (1997): pp.38ff.

Lehrer, E.L. & C.U. Chiswick. "Religion as a Determinant of Marital Stability." *Demography*, 30, (3), (1993): pp.385-402.

Malony, H.N. *Win-Win Relationships: 9 Strategies for Settling Personal Conflicts Without Waging War.* Broadman and Holman Publishers, 1995.

Marriage. "Faith for Today Magazine." Lifestyle Home Seminars, 1991.

Martin, T.C., & L.L. Bumpass. "Recent Trends in Marital Disruption." *Demography*, 26, (1), (February 1989): pp.37-51.

Mayer, R.J. *Conflict Management: The Courage to Confront.* Battelle Press, 1990.

McBurney, L.M. "Treatment for Infidelity Fallout" *(Abstract)*. *Leadership*, 7, (2), (1986): pp.112-119.

_____. "Starting Over: With God's Help, It's Possible to Rebuild Trust-Even after a Painful Betrayal." *Marriage Partnership Magazine*, (No. 2), 15, (Summer 1998): p.32.

McCollough, M.E. "Marital Forgiveness: Theoretical Foundations and an Approach to Prevention. *Marriage & Family: A Christian Journal*, 1, (1), (1997): pp.81-96.

McCullough, M.E., et. al (1998). Interpersonal Forgiving in Close Relationships: II. Theoretical Elaboration and Measurement." *Journal of Personality and Social Psychology*, 1998, 75, (6), pp.1586-1603.

McDowell, J. "Resolving Conflict." *Focus on The Family,* (1993).

Michaud, E. "Discover the Power of Forgiveness." In *Prevention*, 51, i1, (1), (January 1999): p.110.

Mikolaski, S.J. *Encyclopedia of Christian Ethics.* R. K. Harrison (Ed.). Thomas Nelson Publishers (Revised Ed. pp.144-146, 1992.

Murphy, J.G. & Hampton, J. *Forgiveness and Mercy.* Cambridge University Press, 1988.

Nadelhaft, J. "The Englishwoman's Sexual Civil War: Feminist Attitudes Towards Men, Women, and Marriage, 1650-1740." *Journal of the History of Ideas, Inc.* (October 1982): pp.555-590.

Narramore, C.M. *The Psychology of Counseling.* Zondervan Publishing House, 1960.

"National Vital Statistics Reports" (February 25, 1999): 47, (16).

Neal, C. "First Person: Surviving An Affair." *Today's Christian Woman Magazine*, 21, (2), (1999): p.96.

Palmer, R.C. "Contexts of Marriage in Medieval England: Evidence from the king's Court circa 1300." *Speculum*, 59, No. 1. (January 1984): pp.42-67

218

Payn, B., K. Tanfer, O.G. Billy, & W.R. O'Grady. "Men's Behaviour Change Following Infection with a Sexually Transmitted Disease." *Family Planning Perspectives*, 29, (1997): pp.152-157.

Rabior, W. & Leipert. J. *Marriage Makers/Marriage Breakers: Counseling for a Stronger Relationship.* Liguori Publications, Liguori, MO, 1992.

Renker, E. "Wife Beating, and the Written Page." *American Literature*, Vol. 66, No. 1, New Melville. (March 1994): pp.123-15.

Rosen, M.D. "Can This Marriage Be Saved?" *Ladies Home Journal*, (December 1996): pp. 16, 20-22.

Sande, K. *The Peacemaker: A Biblical Guide to Resolving Personal Conflict.* Second ed. Baker Books, 1997.

Sarason, I.S. & B.R. Sarason. *Abnormal Psychology: The Problem of Maladaptive Behaviour.* Eighth ed. Prentice Hall, 1996.

Seamands, D.A. *Healing of Memories: In Healing Your Hearts of Painful Emotions.* Inspirational Press, NY, 1993.

Smedes, L.B. The Art of Forgiving: When You Need To Forgive and Don't Know How. Ballantine Books, 1996.

Smith, T.W. "Adult Sexual Behaviour in 1989: Number of Partners, Frequency of Intercourse, and Risk of AIDS" *Family Planning Perspectives,* 23, (3), (May-June 1991): pp.102-107.

Sohoni, N.K. "The Changing Family and Women's Issues in the 1990s." *Feminists Issues,* 13, (1), (Spring 1993). pp.55 76.

South, S.J., & G. Spitzer. "Determinants of Divorce over the Marital Life Course." *American Sociological Review*, (51), (1986): pp.583-590.

Spring, I A. & M. *After the Affair: Healing the Pain and Rebuilding Trust When a Partner has been Unfaithful.* Harper Collins Publishers, 1993.

Stanley, C. *Put the past behind you and give The Freedom of Forgiveness.* Thomas Nelson Publishers, 1991.

Stitch, S. "When to Forgive Him If He's done the Un-forgiven." *Ladies Home Journal*, (October 1995): pp.94-101.

Texier, C. "Why I Stayed After My Man Strayed: Staying with An Unfaithful Husband." *Cosmopolitan*, 225, (i6), (December 1998): pp.66ff.

The Complete Works of W. Shakespeare. "A Midsummer Night's Dream, Act III, Scene II," p.290. Dorset Press, 1988.

Thomas, D. *The Theology of Marriage, in The New Dictionary of Theology.* J.A. Komonchak, M. Collins, & D.A. Lam, eds. The Liturgical Press, 1991.

Thornton, A., W.G. Axinn, and D.H. Hill. "Reciprocal Effects of Religiosity, Cohabitation, and Marriage." *American Journal of Sociology*, 98, (3), (November 1992): pp.628-651.

Thornton, A. "Changing Attitudes toward Separation and Divorce: Causes and Consequences." *American Journal of Sociology*, 90, (4), (January 1985): pp.856-872.

Toon, P. "Divorce & Remarriage: Their relation to family values, homosexual partnerships and the future of American society." *Discussion Paper* No. 1, (July 1996): Cranmer-Seabury House of Studies.

Tunbridge, J.E. & G.J. Ashworth. "Dissonant Heritage. The Management of the Past as a Resource in Conflict." John Wiley & Sons, 1996.

Vaughan, P. The *Monogamy Myth: A Personal Handbook for Recovering From Affairs.* (New Revised Edition). Copyright © Vaughan & Vaughan, 1999.

Vander Zanden, J.W. *The Social Experience: An Introduction to Sociology.* Random House, 1988.

Warren, N.C. *The Triumphant Marriage.* Focus on the Family Publishing, 1995.

Weiner, M.B. & B.D. Starr. *Stalemates: The Truth about Extramarital Affairs.* New Horizons Press, 1989.

Wiebe, P.H. "Jesus' Divorce Exception." *Journal of The Evangelical Theological Society,* 32, (3), (September 1989): pp.327-333.

Witwer, M. "Marital Instability Grows: Most Recent Marriages in U.S. are Likely to Fail." *Family Planning Perspectives,* 21, (5), (September-October, 1989): pp.234-236.

Worthington, E.L. (Jr.) & F.A. DiBlasio. "Promoting Mutual Forgiveness within the Fractured Relationship." *Psychotherapy,* 27, Summer 1990, (20), (1990): pp.219-223.

Worthington, E.L. (Jr.). *Marriage Counseling: A Christian Approach to Counseling Couples.* Intervarsity Press, 1989.

Zueschner, Raymond. *Communicating Today.* Boston: Allyn and Bacon, 1997.

Appendices

Appendix I
Research Questions

Primary Research Question
"How do Christian wives who remain with their unfaithful husbands resolve interpersonal conflicts" was answered with the use of in-depth questioning, and the explanatory case study protocol approach. Four subsidiary questions emerged from the primary research questions.

Subsidiary Questions

1. What *methods* do Christian wives use to resolve interpersonal conflicts associated with infidelity?
2. Why do Christian wives *remain* with their unfaithful husbands?
3. How do Christian wives deal with the *spiritual, emotional, and psychological* impact of their husband's infidelity?
4. What are some *consequences of infidelity* to Christian wives who remain with their unfaithful husbands?

Data

The descriptive data revealed three main categories namely *spiritual, psychological,* and *emotional*. With the use of grounded theory, these were further subdivided into themes and patterns (see Appendix II, Table I). Appendix III, Table II, shows the relationship of interpersonal conflict to infidelity and the responses of the women to resolve this type of conflict.

Emergent Hypotheses

- Christian wives remain with their unfaithful husbands because they believe they are *obeying the Word of God* by maintaining their marital vows.
- Christian wives *spiritualize* the effects of infidelity and the interpersonal conflicts associated with this behaviour.

Appendix II

Table 1: Showing Emerging Categories and Themes

Categories		
Spiritual	*Psychological*	*Emotional*
Emergent Themes		
• Increased/decreased church attendance • Prayer • Doubts about relationship with God • Forgiveness • Faith • Humility • Overlooking the offense • Overcoming with love • Bible reading • Fasting • Increased church work	• Low self-esteem, self-Worth, and self-concept • Intra-psychic disturbance- confusion, frustration, anxiety, grief, • Cognitive dissonance - Inconsistent thoughts, distortions • Nervousness • Repression • Stress • Depression • Self-pity	• Anger • distancing, • Feelings of betrayal, • Self-blame • Loss of self-respect, self-confidence • Sleeplessness, worry, fear, incessant crying, despair • Feelings of abandonment, loneliness, powerlessness, • Distress, agitation, guilt, hurt, pain, shame, fatigue embarrassment, pride • Sorrow, sadness, bitterness, hostilities

Appendix III

Table 2:
Showing Relationship of Interpersonal Conflict and Infidelity

Responses to Interpersonal Conflict after the Discovery of Infidelity	
• *Jealousy, revenge, contempt, disdain, hatred* • *Threatening to leave* • *Intimacy avoidance* • *Distancing and withdrawal* • *Refusal to talk about the situation* • *Leaving the house or locking oneself in the bedroom.* • *Prayer, Bible reading* • *Attacking the husband* • *Name-calling* • *Trying to solve the problem by silence* • *Poor communication skills to infuriate the husband* • *Talking about the situation and asking the husband about his behaviour in a non-threatening manner* • *Pretending that the problem does not exist or* • *Denial of the problem* • *Spiritualizing the problem, ignoring, or resorting to prayer alone, rather than dealing with the problem* • *An unforgiving attitude, malice, resentment, blaming.* • *Positional, rather than interest-oriented* • *Wife accepts blame for the husband's behaviour and covers it up from others.* • *Making excuses for husband*	• Evidence of win/lose; lose/win; lose/lose • Competitiveness • Compromising • Manipulation and control • Conflict avoidance, flight • Escape • Temptation to fight • Self-righteous attitude • Destructive response to conflict • Verbal abuse and insults • Escalation of conflict leading to outbursts of anger. • Evidence of irritation and frustration • Confrontation • Trying to find meaning for the behaviour of infidelity • Getting outside help • Covering up the existence of problems • Pretending • This is a self-righteousness attitude towards the husband • Escalation of interpersonal conflict • This behaviour will prolong both intra-psychic and interpersonal conflicts • Incessant nagging - competitiveness • This is compromising the behaviour and accepting it as the norm • Over-looking behaviour to keep the peace

Appendix IV
Interview Schedule Questions

(I)   **Background Information**

(a)   How old are you?

(b)   Were you a Christian before you were married?

(c)   Was your husband a Christian at that time?

(d)   Are you active in your church? Tell me about what you do.

(e)   Describe the type of work you do.

(f)   Are you in good health?

(g)   Is there a time when you get together as a family? Explain.

(h)   Do you take vacations together? Explain.

(i)   Do you go out with your husband?

(j)   Has your husband ever asked you not to go to church?

(k)   How did you respond to his request?

(l)   Do you and your husband have an active physical relationship?

(II)   **The Informant's Husband**

(a)   Tell me about your husband. How would you describe him?

(b)   What type of work does he do?

(c)   How does your husband feel about your involvement with the Church?

(d)   Tell me about his relationship with you when you were first married.

(e)   Is your husband in good health?

(f)   Why do you think he was unfaithful towards you?

(III).   **Conflict**

1.   How did you come to know about your husband's adultery?

2.   What was your initial response to the behaviour and to your husband?

3.   What kinds of feelings went through your mind when you found out?

4.   Explain the struggles that you felt.

5.   Were you angry, composed, agitated, or simply hurt. Explain.

6.   What were your decisions after the initial shock?

7.   When did you approach your husband about his infidelity?

8.   How did you confront him?

9.   Where did you confront your husband?

225

10. Were the children present?
11. Were the two of you alone?
12. Did you plan what you were going to say to your husband?
13. Did you accept the behaviour as being your fault or someone else's?
14. How did you respond to the behaviour? Did you ignore it, or block it out? Explain.
15. How did you feel about the interpersonal relationship in the marriage after the exposure, in terms of love, trust, intimacy, and fidelity?
16. Were you fearful about the future of the marriage or of losing your husband?
17. How do you feel about your husband now? Have you forgiven him?

(IV)   Emotions
1. Describe your relationship with God.
2. How do you feel about God now, since your husband's behaviour has not changed over the years.
3. Do you think God is using your husband's infidelity to test your Christian character? Explain.
4. Explain how you felt when you found out about the infidelity.
5. How do you feel now?
6. Describe your relationship with your husband now, in terms of love, trust, and intimacy.
7. How do you feel about yourself?
8. Do you feel a sense of low self-esteem?
9. How do you feel when you are alone?
10. What do you do when you feel depressed?
11. Do you feel powerless at times, and tell yourself that you cannot do anything about your husband's behaviour? Explain this feeling to me.
12. Explain the reasons why you remain with your husband.
13. How do you deal with the feelings of hate, shame, remorse, and embarrassment?
14. You said that you thought about counseling and then changed your mind. Why did you change your mind about that kind of help since according to you, you often felt depressed and discouraged with feelings of rejection?
15. Describe the feeling of revenge that makes you frustrated at times.
16. Do you think you will ever forgive him?
17. How does your answer relate to your belief in God?
18. Why did you not divorce your husband?

Appendix V

Letter to Informants

Date.........................

Dear Participant:

As part of my program towards a doctoral degree in Conflict Management, I am conducting a study on Christian women who are living with husbands who have been unfaithful to them. The purpose of this study is to gain an understanding into why women remain with their husbands, and to find out how they deal with the interpersonal conflict associated with infidelity.

To secure confidentiality, anonymity of you as the respondent, your responses will be protected throughout the study.

Your participation in this study is voluntary, and you can refrain from answering any or all of the questions without explanation. Please note that your responses will be appreciated, and will add to the validity of the study.

It is estimated that your initial participation will take approximately 20-30 minutes for the first session, and this will involve completing the attached waiver form. In essence, the estimated total amount of time for your participation is approximately three hours. I would also like your permission to follow up with a call to you if this is necessary at a day and time convenient for you.

If you have any questions or comments concerning this study, you can contact me at (....................).

Sincerely,

Barbara Stuart

Appendix VI

Human Subjects Research Consent Form

Date ....

I, _____ agree to participate in the research
project being conducted by *Barbara Stuart.*　　　*(Print name in full)*

I understand that excerpts from my report may be quoted in a doctoral study and in future papers, journal articles and books that will be written by the researcher, but without direct identification of my participation.

I grant authorization for the use of the above information with the full understanding that my anonymity and confidentiality will be preserved at all times.

I understand that my full name or other identifying information will never be disclosed or referenced in any written or verbal context. I understand that all transcripts from this report will be secured in the privacy of the researcher's home, and will be destroyed at the end of the project.

I understand that my participation is voluntary, and that I may withdraw my permission to participate in this study without explanation.

I understand that there is no payment for my participation in this research.

_____　　_____
Signature　　　　　　Date

*I waive my right to sign this consent form [   ]

Made in the USA
Charleston, SC
23 July 2010